INNOVATION IN THE BIOPHARMACEUTICAL INDUSTRY

INNOVATION IN THE BIOPHARMACEUTICAL INDUSTRY

EDITORS

RIFAT A. ATUN
Imperial College London, UK

DESMOND SHERIDAN
Imperial College London, UK

NEW JERSEY • LONDON • SINGAPORE • BEIJING • SHANGHAI • HONG KONG • TAIPEI • CHENNAI

Published by

World Scientific Publishing Co. Pte. Ltd.
5 Toh Tuck Link, Singapore 596224
USA office: 27 Warren Street, Suite 401-402, Hackensack, NJ 07601
UK office: 57 Shelton Street, Covent Garden, London WC2H 9HE

Library of Congress Cataloging-in-Publication Data
Innovation in the biopharmaceutical industry / edited by Rifat A. Atun and Desmond Sheridan.
   p. ; cm.
  Includes bibliographical references and index.
  ISBN-13: 978-981-270-660-7 (pbk.)
  ISBN-10: 981-270-660-7 (pbk.)
   1. Pharmaceutical industry--Technological innovations. 2. Pharmaceutical biotechnology. 3.
Biopharmaceuticals. 4. Drug development. I. Atun, Rifat A. II. Sheridan, Desmond J. (Desmond John)
[DNLM: 1. Drug Industry--trends. 2. Delivery of Health Care--trends. 3. Diffusion of Innovation.
4. Health Policy. 5. Technology, Pharmaceutical--trends. QV 736 I58 2007]

RS380.I56 2007
338.4'76151--dc22

                      2007004943

British Library Cataloguing-in-Publication Data
A catalogue record for this book is available from the British Library.

Typeset by Stallion Press
Email: enquiries@stallionpress.com

Printed by FuIsland Offset Printing (S) Pte Ltd, Singapore

CONTENTS

v

ACKNOWLEDGEMENTS

This work was supported by Imperial College and by a grant from Pfizer Corp. In acknowledging this support the authors understand that their responsibility is to assist discussion of issues relating to innovation among the academic, healthcare and general community and that this overrides any obligation to any party who has provided support for the work. We believe we have complied with this responsibility. The opinions expressed are those of the authors and are understood to be subject to normal academic challenge and discourse.

Introduction

INNOVATION IN HEALTH CARE: THE ENGINE OF TECHNOLOGICAL ADVANCES

RIFAT A. ATUN

Centre for Health Management, Tanaka Business School
Imperial College London, South Kensington Campus
London, SW7 2AZ, UK

r.atun@imperial.ac.uk

DESMOND SHERIDAN

Department of Cardiology
National Heart and Lung Institute, Imperial College London
and St Mary's Hospital, Norfolk Place,
London, W2 1PG, UK

d.sheridan@imperial.ac.uk

Better and equitable health is a global aspiration. Health has become a key issue in the development of stable global social, political and economic structures and the creation of mechanisms to achieve it remains one of the greatest challenges we face in the 21st century. Understanding the breath and complexity of the solutions required to improve global health is critical to maintaining substantial progress in this endeavour. Great progress has been made during the past century in understanding diseases, developing new diagnostic technologies and new medicines, resulting in better prevention and treatment of illness and contributing to major advances in longevity in the developed world. Indeed, in the period 1952–1992, over one half of the gains in health were due to access to better technology and application of new knowledge. Remaining gains were due to income improvements and better education (World Health Organization, 1999). However, in spite of these gains the challenges ahead are equally formidable. The emergence of new diseases and the spread of disease as a direct result of human activity or indirectly through environmental change are major new scientific challenges.

The healthcare sector operates in a uniquely complex social, political and ethical environment. All societies recognise the importance of equity in provision of health care and aspire to achieve it through various means, almost always involving a mix of state and private sector involvement. Healthcare systems are characterised by involvement of the state to prevent market failure. The extent of this involvement distinguishes it from other forms of consumption. The involvement of the state in health systems varies in different contexts. It may be limited to "stewardship" of the sector, with an emphasis on regulation, policy development and provision of strategic oversight, or may include involvement in financing, purchasing or delivery of healthcare services. Involvement in healthcare financing may include collection, pooling and allocating resources amassed from the citizens or corporations in the form of taxes, insurance or direct payments. Involvement in service delivery may be direct, with ownership and management of healthcare institutions and employment of the staff who work in these. However, involvement in financing and delivery may be delegated to third parties: public or private "not for profit" or "non-profit distributing" organisations (such as public insurance agencies, non-governmental organisations, trusts or mutuals), or to private "for profit" organisations and structures. However, whatever the mix and the extent of state involvement, all health systems face the challenge of meeting increasing demands that have outgrown the available resources. Understanding the dynamic and complex nature of health systems, and how regulatory interventions help achieve system goals and objectives is critical to designing meaningful policies.

Technological advances and development of new medicines are achieved on the basis of fundamental research carried out in universities and institutes of research, while virtually all end products and medicines are developed and produced by the pharmaceutical and related industries. These organisations operate in markedly differing financial and regulatory environments, but their successful interaction is critical for success. By its nature treatment of disease involves altering or disturbing normal body functions on a temporary or permanent basis to achieve some overall benefit in wellbeing or longevity and therefore necessarily involves some element of risk which is overt and unavoidable. Despite this there appears to be no aspect of human activity which generates a more risk-averse attitude. Huge rates of death and disability are blithely accepted and tolerated in exchange for the pleasures of smoking tobacco and drinking alcohol or the convenience of daily road travel. In contrast we seem to have deluded ourselves into regarding illness as an unjustified inconvenience for which we can expect risk free treatment as a right. As a result the healthcare sector operates in an environment of intense and unique regulation.

Innovation is at the heart of all advances and has the capacity to solve problems facing humanity. Societies which have turned away from innovation and technological development have failed in their ability to support their populations. Understanding the nature of innovation in the life sciences and in particular health care, how it operates, what enables and hinders it is therefore of great importance to meeting the challenges ahead.

Multiple interacting factors influence the uptake and diffusion of new knowledge and technologies which are needed to improve health. In turn, the delivery of health care on a global scale depends on effective and stable political and economic foundations, which have the capacity to improve and manage disease prevention and treatment.

Understanding the nature of innovation in the life sciences is critical to creating innovation ecosystems that combine an appropriate balance of incentives, rewards and regulations that encourage the innovation process but also the uptake and diffusion of innovations once these reach the market place.

Developing such an understanding requires a careful examination of the nature of innovation in the life sciences, the innovation process that spans academic institutions, healthcare systems and multiple industrial organisations, and involves a wide range of stakeholders, as well as the innovation life cycle in the life sciences.

It is all too easy given the complexity and scale of these challenges to focus on single issues and partial solutions that have little prospect of achieving long term gains or which may even hinder solutions in other areas. Hence, policy makers should adopt a holistic approach when developing policies aimed at improving health — informed by sound understanding of the innovation process, knowledge of factors which encourage or hinder innovation, and awareness of the societal expectations which shape the goals and objectives of health systems. Partial understanding of the innovation process, the factors which influence the uptake and diffusion of innovations, and the goals and objectives of health systems may lead to the development of inappropriate policies and partial regulations which hinder the innovation process as well as the uptake and diffusion of innovations.

This book volume, reprinted from the *International Journal of Innovation Management* (Vol. 11, No. 2), brings together a series of papers which address many of the issues related to innovation in the life sciences. The papers, developed by a multidisciplinary group of scholars and practitioners, explore innovation in the life sciences in a holistic manner but viewed through a variety of lenses.

J. Attridge distinguishes theory from practice in managing innovation, as a business and management strategy in the life sciences and in particular in the biopharma sector. He explores how our understanding of innovation has evolved from simple linear "push" and "pull" models to more complex dynamic, interactive incremental ones that more realistically represent what happens in practice.

Using real life case histories, D. Sheridan analyses the innovation process in cardiovascular medicine and illustrates how important advances have emerged. His analysis demonstrates an important feature of the innovation process in the bio-pharma sector: the "bench-to-bedside" interaction. The ability of physicians to work across a wide range of scientific fields at "the bench and bedside" enables continuous innovation, as new technologies and solutions are developed and enhanced incrementally over many years by observing what happens in practice and by building on developing science to address new challenges.

K. Sikora brings a unique practitioner perspective on the importance of innovation in delivering new treatments to patients. His personal view reflects on how innovation may evolve to meet future needs in cancer medicine and outlines the challenges that lie ahead. He argues how within the next 20 years the advances in cancer medicine could transform cancer from a death warrant to long-term health management. But that promise, he contends, depends on sustained investment in innovation, and on the society's willingness to pay for that innovation, but may not be realised in Europe where investment in medical science remains low compared to the United States and where innovation is inadequately rewarded.

Drawing on a review of empirical evidence, R. A. Atun, I. Harvey, and J. Wild stress the critical importance of intellectual property (IP) in enhancing national potential for competitive leadership in the global market for life sciences. Through case studies they illustrate how the US has approached IP strategically and created an IP infrastructure; how Japan aims to develop into an "IP nation"; the way China is investing in creation of a well-developed IP system, while the European Union — which has a fragmented and expensive system of national patents — lacks an environment which values investment in IP generation and management.

R. A. Atun, I. Gurol-Urganci, and D. Sheridan explore how regulatory policies aimed at managing healthcare costs and access to new medical technologies impact on the pace of innovation and health system objectives of equity, efficiency, effectiveness and user choice. They demonstrate an asymmetry between the regulatory policies and efforts to enhance access to new innovative medicines. Often the regulatory policies have too narrow a focus on aggregate measures of efficiency (such as reduction in volume of medicines prescribed or reductions in pharmaceutical budgets), without adequate consideration of the effect on the health system objectives of equity, effectiveness and choice. The complexity and lengthy course of innovation, they argue, makes it hard to evaluate new technologies, as discovering the true benefits of a new medicine may take longer than timing of health technology assessment that determines decisions on adoption of these innovations in health systems. They also note in Europe an undue emphasis on assessing product innovation, but without due concern for process innovations which are introduced without appropriate assessment of benefits. They warn that focusing on short-term efficiency savings in one domain of the health system may have adverse consequences on the system as a whole and recommend decision makers to adopt a more holistic approach to policy making, and to carefully consider the potential impact of regulations on innovation ecosystems, the uptake and diffusion of innovations and the efforts to achieve health system goals.

In the final paper of the series, D. Kleyn, R. I. Kitney, and R. A. Atun explore the role of partnerships between academia and business in fostering innovative technologies. Through a review of published studies and interviews with key informants in the European biopharma, university, and venture capital sectors, the paper identifies perceived benefits of partnering, strategies pursued by organisations engaged in research partnerships and the factors which encourage or hinder the development of successful partnerships. Although biopharma R&D partnering activity in the UK and some other European countries is encouraged there are few studies which assess the benefits of these interventions in the European context and empirical evidence is lacking. While the views of key informants differ on the adequacy of current government support for industry–university research partnerships in the UK, there is agreement on the key barriers to developing healthy partnerships, which include pressure on pricing from industry partners; asymmetry of experience, knowledge, and skills between industry and universities; problems with negotiating ownership of IP; and excessive bureaucracy coupled with lack of administrative support from universities.

Collectively, these studies demonstrate the critical importance of taking a holistic view of innovation from "concept to diffusion" or from "bench to bedside" when developing health and science policy. The dangers of partial understanding of the innovation process or well intentioned but narrow assessment of the value of innovations are all too obvious. The critical importance of seeing the innovation process, as distinct from the products it produces, as an invaluable engine of technological advance is not yet adequately appreciated in the European context, where the rewards for the innovator to encourage investments needed to sustain research and development are inadequate or mistargeted. Indeed, a recent review of research funding in the UK has highlighted poor coordination of research funding and suboptimal collaboration amongst key organisations engaged in the innovation process (Cooksey, 2006). But as the studies in this volume demonstrate, these problems are not confined to the UK but are prevalent in Europe which faces a decline in academic clinical science (Sheridan, 2006).

Until recently, the EU enjoyed global competitive advantage in the life sciences. This advantage has been lost and the research to inform us on the reasons for this decline are lacking. One could argue that perhaps Europe's decline as a creative force in the health and bioscience sectors results not from what is happening in the laboratory, but from policies and practices built on a misunderstanding of the innovation process itself. To regain this competitive advantage the EU must invest substantially in R&D, IP generation and commercialisation of these outputs. However, these investments must be coupled with policies that encourage interaction amongst all the key parties involved in innovation and reward innovation along the whole innovation cycle.

References

Attridge, J (2007). Innovation models in the biopharmaceutical sector. *International Journal of Innovation Management*, 11(2).

Atun, RA, I Gurol-Urganci and D Sheridan (2007a). Uptake and diffusion of pharmaceutical innovations in health systems. *International Journal of Innovation Management*, 11(2).

Atun, RA, I Harvey and J Wild (2007b). Innovation, patents and economic growth. *International Journal of Innovation Management*, 11(2).

Cooksey, D (2006). *A Review of UK Health Research Funding*. London: Stationery Offi ce.

Kleyn, D, RI Kitney and RA Atun (2007). Partnerships and innovation in the life sciences. *International Journal of Innovation Management*, 11(2).

Sheridan, D (2006). Reversing the decline of academic medicine in Europe. *The Lancet*, 367(9523), 1698–1701.

Sheridan, D (2007). Development and innovation in cardiovascular medicine. *International Journal of Innovation Management*, 11(2).

Sikora, K (2007). Development and innovation in cancer medicine. *International Journal of Innovation Management*, 11(2).

World Health Organization (1999). The World Health Report 1999. Geneva: WHO.

INNOVATION MODELS IN THE BIOPHARMACEUTICAL SECTOR

JIM ATTRIDGE

Centre for Health Management
Tanaka Business School, South Kensington Campus
SW7 2AZ London, UK
jimattridge@aol.com

The innovation process in the biopharmaceutical sector is influenced by long business cycles, multiple stakeholders and complex interactions. Early models of the innovation process are inadequate to capture the complexity of innovation in the life sciences sector. In particular, narrow classifications which describe innovations as "radical" or "incremental" are not particularly useful when considered in the context of the complex patterns of interrelated innovations observed in practice.

Many partial models of the innovation process which equate innovation to inventive research, patenting and product development fail to recognise that innovation is a cyclical and business-driven process and underscore the final phase of the innovation process, namely, achieving timely market diffusion and adoption of innovations to benefit patients and innovators. Innovation is sustained if it is appropriately rewarded. Investment in the science base alone without appropriate reward system for innovations is unlikely to promote renewed competitiveness in the European biopharmaceutical industry.

Keywords: Innovation; models; biopharmaceuticals; Europe; competitiveness.

General Models of Innovation

A large body of evidence strongly links innovation to economic growth. (Schumpeter, 1934; Baumol, 2002) Therefore, it is not surprising, that governments in developed countries are making strong efforts to promote innovation.

Early models regarded innovation as a linear process: a sequence of activities driven either by "technology push" (basic advances in knowledge) or "market pull" (social or economic opportunities that provide an incentive for risk-taking investment to seek new solutions). Later models recognised that success was highly

1

dependent on coupling these two forces together (see Tidd, 2006 for a detailed discussion).

The relative value of "radical", "incremental" and "imitative" new products, is currently at the heart of a vigorous debate in the biopharmaceutical sector. More recent research has focussed attention on the inherent dangers of basing government policies, or corporate strategies on limited or partial models which fail to recognise key features and interactions in the innovation process (Tidd *et al.*, 2005). Thus, models which portray innovations only as major "breakthroughs" ignore the value of incremental advances.

A central theme in Schumpeter's economic theory of innovation was "creative destruction" (Schumpeter, 1934). Abernathy and Utterback (1985) developed a "discontinuous" model, in which there is an initial "fluid phase", marked by high uncertainty along the "target" and "technical" dimensions. The key uncertainty along the target dimension relates to what the new configuration will look like and who will want the innovation that emerges. The technical dimension relates to the way new technological knowledge is harnessed to create and deliver innovation.

No one knows what will be the "right" configuration of technological approach and market needs, and so there is extensive experimentation, accompanied by many failures, but there is also rapid learning by a range of players, including new entrepreneurial entrants. Gradually, this experimentation converges around a "dominant design", which resets the rules of the game: this is what has happened in the transition from chemical to biological approaches to developing new medicines.

Many of the existing players are able to build on this new trajectory. By leveraging their accumulated knowledge, networks, skills and financial assets, they are able to enhance their competence by building on this new opportunity (Tushman and Anderson, 1987). Equally, while small entrepreneurial firms play an important role in this early phase, there is strong ecological pressure on new entrants, with the result that only the fittest or luckiest survive. This paper will illustrate the importance of these ideas later on, when we analyse the evolving symbiotic relationship between big pharmaceutical companies and small-to-medium sized enterprises (SMEs) that are active in the field of biotechnology.

There is growing evidence that networking is a beneficial mode of operation in innovation. Table 1 provides a summary of the many types of innovation networks and the ways they are used.

Systems theory demonstrates that networks have emergent properties, i.e. the whole is greater than the sum of all its parts. This approach, in which having the right connections becomes as important as the actual generation and ownership of knowledge, has been called "open innovation" by Chesborough (2003).

Table 1. Typology of innovation networks.

Type of innovation network	Primary purpose/innovation target
New product or process development consortium	Sharing knowledge and perspectives to create and market new product or process concepts
Sectoral forum	Shared concern to adopt and develop innovative best practices
Technology consortiums	Sharing and learning around newly emerging technologies
Emerging standards	Exploring and establishing standards around innovative technologies
Clusters	Regional grouping of companies to exploit innovation synergies

Appropriating the Value of Innovation

Innovation creates value which is shared between stakeholders. Teece (1987) argues that, over the long run, four parties share the value generated by innovations: customers, innovators, imitators and other followers. Frequently, the customer can be adjudged to have been the most substantial beneficiary. The extent to which the innovator captures value will depend upon how long the innovation can be protected from imitators, i.e. its sustainability, which, in turn, depends not only upon the legal mechanisms for intellectual property (IP) protection (patents, trademarks and copyrights), but also upon the complexity and ownership of tacit knowledge and the skills required to exploit it.

Comparative analyses have demonstrated a wide variation in the extent to which formal IP protection is essential for enabling the innovator to capture value (Mansfield, 1986). Pharmaceuticals have always emerged from these studies as the sector that is most dependent upon formal patent protection.

The commercialisation process is also vitally important to appropriation. Manufacturing, distribution and marketing of new products all involve specialist complementary assets, which are important in determining appropriability and sustainability and not readily available to imitators. Global marketing reach is the essential complement to intensive R&D investment in many "high tech" sectors, including pharmaceuticals.

Diffusion and Adoption of Innovations

The diffusion of an innovation is typically described by an S-shaped (logistic) curve. Initially, the rate of adoption is low, and confined to "innovators". Next come the "early adopters", then the "late majority", and finally, with the "laggards" the curve tails off (Rogers, 1962).

Research on the rate and extent of the adoption of an innovation — the diffusion rate — has identified a number of factors which affect diffusion (Dosi, 1992). Among others, they include:

- *Relative advantage or value*: the degree to which an innovation is perceived as better than competing products.
- *Compatibility*: the degree to which an innovation is perceived to be consistent with the existing values, experience and needs of potential adopters.
- *Complexity*: the degree to which an innovation is perceived as being difficult to use or understand.
- *Trialability*: the degree to which an innovation can be experimented with on a limited basis. An innovation that is trialable represents less uncertainty for potential adopters, and allows for "learning by doing".
- *Observability*: the degree to which the results of an innovation are visible to others. The easier it is for others to see the benefits of an innovation, the more likely it is to be adopted.

Distinguishing Features of the Biopharmaceutical Sector and Its Environment

Economic growth through innovation has become the watchword of governments. Advances in bioscientific knowledge and their application in medicine by the biopharmaceutical sector, is seen by many as the epitome of this type of sector (Baumol, 2002). This "knowledge-industry" complex has a number of distinguishing features defining both its *modus operandi* and its near environment. For example, (1) The World Health Organization has argued that good health through equal access to the best available healthcare is a human right, and that medical knowledge is a "public good" which should be free from proprietary ownership rights; (2) There is a widely held view that patients should have equal access to medicines, regardless of ability to pay for them. But under market regulation, particularly in competition law, the biopharmaceutical sector is regarded as a private, for-profit sector just like any other; (3) Increasingly refined systems of technical legislation have evolved to ensure that medicines will only be licensed for commercialisation as long as they meet stringent standards of efficacy, safety and quality; (4) Long experience suggests that, in practice, the biopharma innovation model is critically dependent upon strong IP rights, especially in the form of patents (Mansfield, 1986).

Within this short list lie the seeds of much conflict and confusion regarding the nature of biopharmaceutical innovation, decisions about who should manage it, and mechanisms to ensure a fair balance in appropriating the value it creates. A number of policy issues flow from the interplay of these considerations. As we go forward, the extent to which these issues can be resolved will determine the sustainability of the current innovation model. These issues include:

1. What share of public funds for academic and associated scientific and medical research should be allocated to bioscience in any given country?
2. How should R&D investment be prioritised, given all the diverse global health challenges?
3. When setting standards for data on efficacy, safety and quality, how might we best achieve a balance between benefit and risk for patients while still ensuring that the cost of development for innovators is not prohibitive?
4. How should national patent systems and global patent conventions evolve to strike a balance between maximising public access to useful new medicines, and ensuring that returns earned during the period of patent protection provide incentives for further R&D investment?
5. What approaches will assess the value of new products over their market life cycle?
6. How can we best achieve a fair and reasonable approach to price differentials between different population segments both within and across countries?

Each of these issues has been the subject of debate which often has led to major conflicts between stakeholders. The conflict is not only due to different social and economic values, but also to a lack of common understanding about the nature of the innovation process. The following sections examine the limitations of partial models in the context of changing industry dynamics and government policies and regulation.

Partial Innovation Models in the Biopharmaceutical Sector

In their landmark text on pharmaceutical innovation, Landau *et al.* (1999) chart the progress of innovation in the 20th century and provide an accessible account of the changes in science, medicine and commerce, all of which have combined to deliver great advances in therapeutics. In addition, Achilladelis and Antonakis (2001) have chronicled the growth of national pharmaceutical industries in the US, Europe and Japan. Through their global reach, "machine like" product development competences, and efficient integration of these two attributes, these countries and regions have become today's industry leaders.

In both of these accounts, multiple coupling of the "technology push" and "market pull" effects is apparent (Rothwell, 1992a). In its early years the pharmaceutical industry was dominated largely by "technology push". Achilladelis and Antonakis (2001) charted progress over several decades and placed considerable emphasis upon the parallel development of clusters of innovations across the entire field of medicine, physiology, diagnostic techniques and equipment, advances in human biology, chemistry and other pharmaceutical sciences.

In practice, the *modus operandi* of the pharmaceutical sector has been characterised by four component parts:

1. Bioscience and medical knowledge creation, from fundamental advances in our understanding of molecular and cellular structures and processes, to improved knowledge of disease aetiology and treatment protocols in medical practice.
2. Advances in knowledge which has original and potentially useful applications which can be patented.
3. Presence of a secure patent position, enabling biopharmaceutical companies to commit to the long-term, high-risk, high-expense development process. If successful, this culminates in a dossier for regulatory approval.
4. The ability to rapidly commercialise the product across world markets and achieve a commercial return commensurate with the scale of investment and associated risks.

Figure 1 shows an early linear model of innovation in the pharmaceutical sector. The figure illustrates the sequential nature of the process, whereby these events take place, and also the high level of interaction with external agencies and regulatory systems. The continuing evolution of this process has been largely driven by three factors: (1) advances in scientific and medical knowledge; (2) a need to ensure that medicines are safe, effective, and of good quality; (3) the need for companies investing in R&D over the long-term to achieve a profitable return.

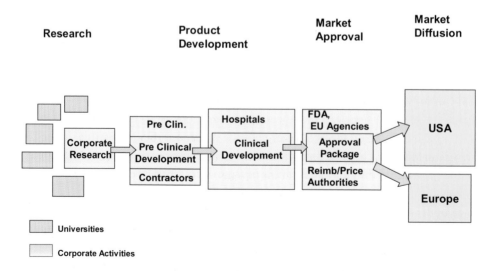

Fig. 1. A linear model of pharmaceutical innovation prior to 1990.

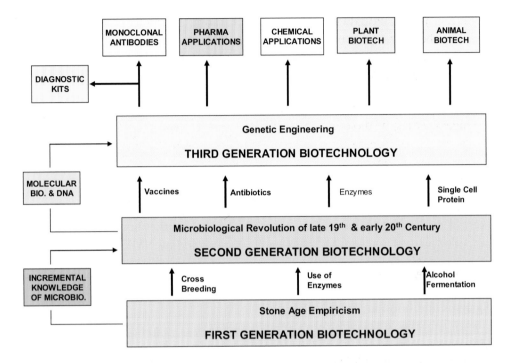

Fig. 2. Long waves of bioscience innovation. *Source*: After Sharpe M. *et al.* (1994)

The second of these factors, namely the constant upgrading of government agency standards to ensure the safety and efficacy of new products, has had a major impact on the pharmaceutical innovation process. The changing regulatory environment, with more stringent safety and efficacy requirements, has prompted the pharmaceutical industry to respond with sophisticated strategies for managing the R&D process more efficiently, and submitting final dossiers for new products in time for regulatory approval. These strategies include the development of new capabilities based on interdisciplinary teamwork, as well as highly specialised competences for managing the innovation process across an international array of contributors. This approach exemplifies a progression towards Rothwell's (1992a) "four generation" model. However, despite the efficiency gains that have been achieved, the time from conception to market has changed little over the past 20 years (8–12 years), while the costs of development have continued to escalate (Di Masi, 2003).

There is now a trend towards more sophisticated links to external suppliers and customers. "In-house" pre-clinical and clinical development activities now involve clusters of external research contractors, clinical research management organisations and clinical research units in hospitals.

Advances in the fundamental understanding of bioscience at the molecular level in recent years have all the hallmarks of a "technological revolution". Sharpe *et al.*

(1994) characterised the evolution of biotechnology as a process involving three successive waves of such changes, as shown in Fig. 2.

Although research within the third bio-molecular wave has been underway for over two decades (Sharpe *et al.*, 1994), experience of long waves of industrial development suggests that this massive new knowledge base will translate slowly and unevenly into practical innovations. Many people are frustrated by the slow rate at which new knowledge translates into innovations, especially in the face of social and economic pressures for better treatments of serious diseases, such as cancer, rheumatoid arthritis, Alzheimer's and AIDS. (Nightingale and Martin, 2004) Simple coupling models, though useful as a starting point, offer no guarantees of timely success.

We are faced by a paradoxical situation. The long-term potential at the "front end" of the innovative process appears to be bright, but the short-term innovative output of new products at the "back end", as measured by NME licenses granted, continues to decline (Charles River Associates, 2004).

Systems and boundaries

Systemic models offer a valuable way to order and structure innovative processes. A key feature of the definition of any system is its boundaries. What is within the system as an interactive component, and what is outside and hence part of its external environment? Differing concepts regarding the identification of the component parts of the innovation process and how widely the boundaries are set can lead to quite different conclusions.

The word innovation offers considerable scope for alternative interpretations. Consider the following three definitions:

1. Innovation is the process of discovering something that is both new and potentially useful.
2. Innovation is the process of discovering something new and developing it into a saleable product or service.
3. Innovation is a cyclical economic process, whereby innovators discover, develop and commercialise new products or services and gain sufficient returns on their investments to re-invest in continued R&D.

In the public policy debate on bioscience, the first definition above, which, strictly speaking, refers to "invention", is commonly used to define "innovation". This can lead to the erroneous view that all that is needed to promote innovation is to stimulate more basic scientific and technological inventions; this is a commonly shared view within the EU context. Even in the specialist literature, the innovation process is often limited to the discovery, development and manufacturing processes as in the second definition above, with marketing activities and competences seen as complementary assets. Such an outlook can have the unfortunate result of fostering a view that for this sector, market diffusion through educational information programmes and marketing, is just an "optional extra" rather than, as in the third definition above, an essential, integral part of the innovation process.

Similarly, in business models which are used both for decision making in the industry and for evaluating the impact of government policies and regulation, there is scope for setting systems' boundaries at different levels. Hence, there are different ways to define innovation and business models, depending on the boundaries chosen. These will be explored further below.

Classification models

Freeman (1982) proposed a classification system based upon degrees of innovation — revolutionary, radical or incremental — as shown in Table 2. Many have drawn on this typology to describe pharmaceutical innovations. For example, the term "revolutionary" innovations can be used to describe major conceptual advances such as the identification of microbes and classes of anti-infection agents, which emerged in the second long-term bio-wave.

The distinction between "radical" and "incremental" innovations offers a convenient approach to making more subtle distinctions. For example, a new understanding of a disease mechanism and a new mode of action which interferes with the disease process at a molecular level can be described by the term "radical" innovation. Within this envelope, however, alternative molecules developed with different attributes, which offer value in treating particular disease variants or patient segments, can be referred to by the term "incremental" innovation.

In practice, based upon different patterns of patent ownership, companies simultaneously engage in a competitive race to develop new products which all have the same mode of action (Landau *et al.*, 1999). This makes it difficult to use the terms "radical" and "incremental" to distinguish between individual products. The entry

Table 2. Types of biopharmaceutical innovations.

Radical	Revolutionary
New disease treatment mechanisms and families of closely related chemical or biological products	Major therapeutic models e.g. anti-infectives based on biotechnology
Incremental	Technology system change
Individual new products and formulation variants	IT based pharma R&D systems, Genetic profiling, modern ITC systems, diagnostics

to market of the first product in a new class is followed by a number of other products offering alternative therapeutic and side effect profiles. The resulting market includes a competitive class of products that have a range of variable attributes. For patients, however, the third, fourth or fifth class entrant may offer a better balance of therapeutic benefits to side-effect risks than the first.

A number of options exist for using these terms correctly. For example, the first product in a new class to market might be called the "radical" innovation while all those following are labelled "incremental" innovations. Alternatively, the term "radical" might be used to describe the class as a whole, reflecting the collective effort of the range of players involved in the process, and all the products would be referred to as "incremental" alternatives. The term "radical" is thus reserved for the process, while the term "incremental" is used for individual products. A third, *ex-poste* option is to label the clinical consensus view of the best in the class as the "radical" innovation.

Such niceties of terminology are not merely of academic interest. These distinctions play a critical role in shaping the policies of large state purchasers who use such classifications to determine whether or not they will reimburse a new product and at what price. Products designated as "incremental" innovations might not be adequately reimbursed, and hence have little or no chance of achieving significant sales revenues.

A more extreme approach to classification is to label products as either "breakthrough" or "me-too". This approach labels the first product to market as the "breakthrough" and all later entrants as "me-too's" (Morgan *et al.*, 2005). Such a crude approach to classification would appear to be inconsistent with the substantial body of evidence which demonstrates that this is not the case. Studies by Wells (1988), Kettler (1998), Gelijns (1998), and most recently Di Masi and Paquette (2004) show that later members of a product class frequently are acknowledged by clinicians as the best all-round product in the class. R&D on these products provides a platform for more diverse innovations, such as extended indications, new treatments for other diseases, and more effective formulations.

The way these distinctions are used in markets to determine rewards for innovators sends important signals to the managers who set priorities in R&D.

Business, Portfolio and Product Lifecycle Models

Business models and corporate strategy

Redwood (1987) drew attention to the growing intensity of competition in R&D and international product class markets. He introduced the concept of the "investment–innovation cycle" — a simplified version of which is shown in Fig. 3.

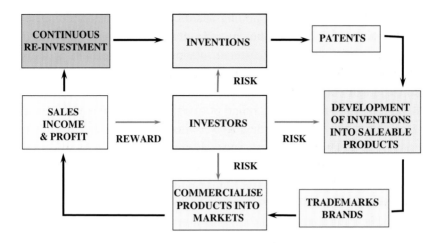

Fig. 3. The "investment–innovation" cycle.

This model places the modern integrated company at the centre of a cycle of "risk-taking" investment decisions. Such risk-taking, if successful, culminates in revenues and profits that can, in part, be distributed to reward investors and in part reinvested in further R&D activities. This model also shows that achieving a sound patent position is a critical step.

Despite the current interest in "public-private" partnership models for pharmaceutical innovation, the output of innovative products over the past 50 years has been almost exclusively generated by large multinational pharmaceutical companies. This is not to suggest that the model is immutable. Currently, there is a growing concern regarding the decline in productivity of established companies (Charles River Associates, 2004). The growing cadre of bioscience-based new entrants may successfully lead the way to the adoption of more efficient business models for accessing international markets. Corporate strategies determine the level of a company's overall investment in R&D, and the allocation of resources across technologies and therapeutic classes. In recent years, investment in inter-company alliances and contract research beyond the traditional boundaries of a company has grown substantially, both in an attempt to sustain revenue streams and profitability, and to ensure long-term stability of the corporate platform on which innovation occurs. Such alliances also influence the share price of publicly listed companies, as the commercial potential of product pipelines becomes increasingly influential in the comparative valuations of companies (Adkins *et al.*, 2003).

R&D investment and portfolio models

R&D strategy defines the disease areas where investments will be made and the proportion of total expenditure that will go to each of these areas. These strategic decisions are long-term because building necessary capabilities to compete effectively in a given disease sector takes many years. It involves bringing together diverse scientific expertise, facilities and external relationships that cannot be transferred from one disease sector to another.

Pharmaceutical companies continually assess the scientific, medical and commercial viability of a portfolio of around 50–100 projects. Some of these are high-risk, with a low probability of leading to a commercial product, while others offer more immediate prospects of return. Some projects will be in the earliest stages of the 8 to 12-year time-line from early research to market approval (Fig. 4), while others will be closer to market entry. Managing the balance of this portfolio over time requires a sophisticated mix of project evaluation techniques, experience and risk-taking judgements.

Individual product strategy and life cycle models

Individual product development projects are undertaken by interdisciplinary teams whose composition changes over time as it moves forward. Successful completion of the innovation cycle requires major contributions from disciplines beyond R&D, most notably, manufacturing and marketing experts. Life cycle models of the type illustrated in Fig. 4 are widely used within companies and by business sector analysts and academics (Adkins *et al.*, 2003; Grabowski and Vernon, 2000; Pammolli *et al.*, 2003) to evaluate returns on individual products, and to balance expenditures against income and calculate net present values. The long timescale of over 30 years makes the accumulation of data a major challenge for retrospective analyses. In the R&D portfolio context, making forecasts of future revenues is largely a conjectural exercise.

Despite these difficulties, invaluable insights into patterns of life cycle returns have been achieved (Grabowksi and Vernon, 2000) which will be discussed further below.

The "big pharma" – SME – academia interface

In a cross-industry study of the role that small firms have played in innovation between 1945 and 1980, Rothwell (1984) observed that, unlike other sectors, SMEs had made little or no contribution to innovation in the pharmaceutical sector. In a similar study covering the 1980s Patel and Pavitt (1994; Patel, 1995) noted that the traditional "academia-industry" research model, illustrated in Fig. 1, had evolved into a more complex three-part model, in which small "spin-off" companies and SMEs had played a more prominent role in the innovation process. In part, this might be attributable to the large pool of tacit knowledge created in the biomolecular wave that was being transmitted from academia to the established large firms.

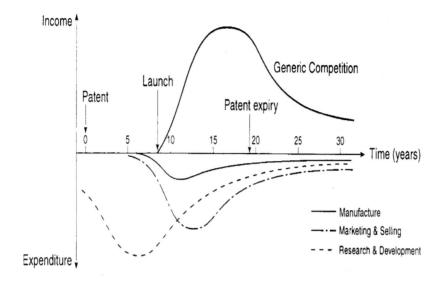

Fig. 4. Typical "investment–income" profile for a single product.

The capability to patent potentially useful new knowledge was dramatically upgraded in universities during the 1980s and 1990s and played a major role in facilitating this new form. A more pro-active approach to patent protection and equity participation in "start-up" companies was adopted by universities and supported by mixed public funding and venture capital. These were important factors which encouraged the creation of "spin-off" companies.

Zucker and Darby (1997) studied how one leading pharmaceutical company transformed its R&D by developing biological drug-design capabilities. New competences were developed by hiring scientists with bioscience skills and establishing a corporate ethos of continual transformation.

Rothaermel (2001) and Rothaermel and Deeds (2004) have analysed alliances between small biotech and "big pharma" companies in the USA and concluded that incumbent big pharma companies exhibit a preference for alliances that leverage complementary biotech assets for commercial exploitation (exploitation alliances) over alliances that focus on building new technological competences (exploration alliances). Biotechnology firms which focus on product technologies depend on big pharma firms to take them forward into clinical development. However, firms that have platform technologies rely on a broader range of network relationships which tend to be less secure (Orsenigo *et al.*, 2001).

Figure 5 summarises the primary relationships in pharmaceutical R&D as it exists today. The smaller intermediaries often have a short and tenuous existence as creators of IP, which they sell to the major pharmaceutical companies at some stage of early development. In Europe, few of these intermediaries have achieved

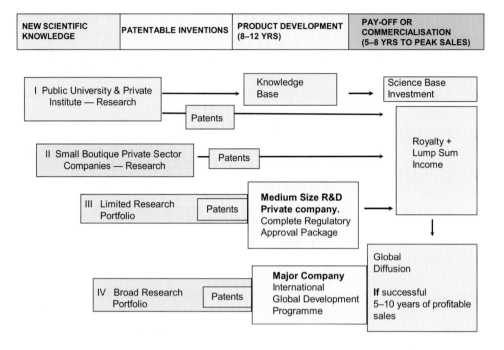

Fig. 5.   R&D relationships in innovation networks.

the critical mass and the funding necessary to run clinical trial programmes. Pisano (2006) in a comprehensive review of the evolution of the US biotech sector has highlighted that in aggregate SMEs have generated spectacular revenue growth, but profitability has remained at very low levels compared to the pharmaceutical sector as a whole. Attrition rates through bankruptcy or merger and acquisition remain high.

Thus far, relatively little research is available on how the contractual arrangements between this more complex set of players shares the actual, or potential future rewards for innovators.

Innovation networks and clusters in biopharmaceuticals

A large body of research has been encouraged by governments to identify new organisational forms that might help enhance global competitiveness through innovation. It explores the merits of different organisational forms and relationships (Bailey *et al.*, 1994). A major set of OECD studies has been published recently, which document and compare national systems for biopharmaceutical innovation (OECD, 2006). Much attention has been focussed upon the evolution of both large and small academic research centres situated in small geographical clusters, and associated knowledge networks in the USA.

The publications and patents produced by tightly knit geographical communities of academia, SMEs, and large pharmaceutical companies (e.g. in New England and California), as well as the benefits gained for these groups, have all been studied extensively. Pammolli *et al.* (2002) have analysed the efforts of European countries to replicate this phenomenon by selectively deployment of government and EU Commission research funds. Kettler and Casper (1998) have documented early initiatives of this type in Germany and the UK. While the UK biotechnology sector has made modest progress, in Germany and other continental countries such efforts have thus far met with only limited success. Such shortcomings may, in part, reflect structural differences in the industries of these countries which have a residue of medium-sized pharmaceutical companies not sufficiently research-intensive to act as effective local partners (McKelvey *et al.*, 2003).

A US study of 94 biotechnology start-ups (Deeds *et al.*, 2000) found that three factors were associated with success: (1) location within a significant concentration of similar firms; (2) quality of scientific staff (measured by citations); (3) the commercial experience of the founder. The number of alliances appeared to have no significant impact on success. However, George *et al.* (2002) have observed that close association of small firms with academic centres enhanced patent output.

A distinct stream of research has examined the role of entrepreneurs. Baumol (2006) has highlighted the "invisibility" of the entrepreneur in contemporary economic models. He also offers the intriguing view that major innovations periodically generated by entrepreneurial researchers reflect a wilful determination, or a bounded rationality, not to acknowledge the excessively long odds against achieving success. In a similar vein, Audretsch *et al.* (2006) studied the prevalence and determinants of the commercialisation of research by university scientists funded by the US National Cancer Institute. They commented that "scientific entrepreneurship is the sleeping giant of commercialising university research. More than one in four patenting NCI scientists in the US has started a new firm".

There is substantial disagreement over the extent to which the EU innovation deficit is caused by lack of venture capital (VC) funding (Daily Telegraph, 2006). Robb (2006) concluded that Europe has attracted less institutional VC than the US, because European entrepreneurs generate fewer projects in the life sciences and information technology that fit within the VCs' investment strategy. He also speculates that because entrepreneurial activity within institutionally backed start-ups is smaller by orders of magnitude than entrepreneurial activity within large firms, more might be learned about why corporatist Europe lags in terms of innovation, by examining the behaviour of established companies.

Diffusion and Adoption of Medicines

The final critical phase in the biopharmaceutical innovation process is the timely introduction of new medicines into general usage. The substantial literature on this topic can be broadly divided into three categories:

1. The impact of complex and changing patterns of demand- side decision makers country by country.
2. Variation in diffusion rates across international markets.
3. The growing use of formal health technology assessment (HTA) processes to manage the selective uptake of new products.

Demand side decision making

Bhide (2006) in a broadly-based comparative analysis of innovative activity in Europe and the USA strongly argues that US superior competitiveness is more likely to be attributable to the greater willingness of US consumers, relative to their European counterparts, to try out and then adopt innovations, than to differences in public policies promoting academic science, the output of science graduates, or the environment for industrial R&D.

In the biopharmaceutical sector the dynamic relationship on the demand side between the three primary customer groups (doctors, payers and patients), results in complex patterns of decision making which determine the uptake of new medicines.

Historically, within OECD markets doctors have been the dominant decision makers, and innovative suppliers have looked primarily to them to achieve rapid diffusion. However, in the 1990s, payers, mainly state insurance budget holders, adopted a far more assertive role in decision making through cost management systems and through the direct involvement of clinicians in budget holding. Payer led cost containment has become a major feature of healthcare systems in Europe and has had a major impact on medicines' expenditure.

Typical features of initiatives which influence diffusion rates are:

1. National guidelines limiting usage to only selected patient categories.
2. Limiting usage to a narrow range of indications.
3. Non-reimbursement of the product from state system funds or high levels of patient co-payment.
4. Budget capped formulary lists limiting access or expenditure.
5. Diverse forms of direct product price controls.

Currently, there are numerous initiatives aimed at giving patients more choices in terms of treatment regimens. The nature and the pace of change vary greatly by disease segment, by country and by access to information technologies such as the internet.

The rapid uptake in the US of new treatments for heart disease, osteoarthritis, and Alzheimer's disease has, in part, been attributed to these new channels of communication. Berndt (2003) has shown this form of communication to have increased the overall diffusion of some product classes, though it would appear to have had little impact on the respective market shares of individual companies. In Europe and Japan, the pace of change is slower and the medical professions have reservations about the implications for the "doctor–patient" relationship.

International comparisons of diffusion rates

Regardless of the sophistication of the models deployed, decades of general consumer research supports Rogers' model of diffusion, in which a substantial range of behaviours causes variable uptake rates for innovations in large populations. Research strongly suggests that this model applies equally well to the uptake of medicines by doctors, healthcare payers and patients, and leads to typical "S-shaped" diffusion curves. Although in principle, modern state systems are expected to rapidly build and communicate a consensus view on the value and appropriate use of new products, this is not what is reflected in the results of empirical uptake studies that have taken place over many years.

Parker (1984) demonstrated very large differences when he compared average time-lags and mean sales for a range of modern medicines in developed countries between 1954 and 1971. A more recent analysis (Cambridge Pharma Consulting, 2002) of a wide range of products shows that major differences persist, despite more efficient and consistent national licensing systems and more effective marketing by leading companies in OECD countries.

Danzon and Kim (2002) compared lifecycle revenues, volumes and prices for a group of 196 globally available molecules in Canada, France, Germany, Italy, Japan and the US between 1981 and 1992. The authors concluded that diffusion was particularly rapid in France, Canada and the US, but much slower in Germany and the UK.

In a broad ranging study addressing epidemiological data on patient access to the best available new therapies across many disease sectors and classes of medicines, Schoffski (2002) highlighted widespread delays in adoption across EU countries, even for therapies which had been available for many years. A recent study of the uptake of modern anti-cancer medicines in EU countries by Jonsson and Wilking (2005) confirms large differences in adoption between countries.

A number of factors contribute to these observations. First, based on long standing differences in national medical cultures and traditions, evidence suggests that there are substantial differences in clinicians' attitudes towards new products (Payer, 1989). For example, Griffin (1985) has noted the "therapeutic conservatism" of UK doctors in adopting innovative medicines compared to doctors in France, Italy and Spain. Recently, the growing influence of budget holding payers in many European countries appears to have had a negative impact both on time to market entry, and on the rate of diffusion of innovative product classes such as statins (Walley *et al.*, 2004).

Recent studies have highlighted that the bureaucratic delays which exist in national approval systems, and the delays which occur during the negotiation of state-reimbursed prices, can both be significant barriers to the uptake of new innovations in Europe (Cambridge Pharma, Consulting, 2002).

Diffusion models and health technology assessment

There is considerable debate concerning the role of HTA methodologies in the prospective evaluation of the potential value of innovations, and its impact on diffusion. In the UK, the National Institute of Clinical Excellence (NICE) has taken a leading role in formally assessing new products' clinical and cost effectiveness before market entry, highlighting "best value for money". A key aim of NICE is achieving uniformity of practice across the UK NHS. However, recent studies have cast doubt as to the feasibility and effectiveness of this initiative (Attridge, 2006; Kings Fund, 2006).

From the industry's perspective, there is concern that HTA methodologies will not adequately recognise the value of the bulk of its output, namely, incremental advances. Even for major new classes, which in retrospect clearly constitute radical progress, pre-launch assessment can delay entry into markets or slow diffusion. Such a situation was recently apparent in the UK with the anti-cancer drug Herceptin.

Appropriability and sustainability in biopharmaceuticals

It is difficult to define the value of a medical innovation and to estimate how it is shared between many different stakeholders. *Ex-poste* historical studies provide a limited guide regarding the scale of benefits that accrue. Dramatic improvements in the treatment of infectious disease, heart disease, mental illness, AIDS, and even cancer have benefited both patients and society. The pharmaceutical industry has all the while been able to sustain profitable growth and to reward well both employees and investors.

Two questions dominate research in this area:

1. How should governments seek to set the balance between the social and economic value of the biopharmaceutical industry's output, and the rewards for its innovative activities?

2. What is the relationship between government interventions that contain expenditure on medicines and industry willingness to continue investing in R&D?

In US based studies, Lichtenberg (2005) found that new medicines launched between 1980 and 2000 contributed substantially to increasing patients' lifespans, and reducing expensive hospital stays. In a series of papers based largely upon experience in the US, Scherer (2004) explored various economic models for setting the balance between innovative progress and affordability of medicines. He concluded that although there exists a need to carefully track the effects of patent protection along with the forces of market competition, direct government regulations on pricing would be counterproductive over the long term. Such US models are instructive because the US represents approximately half of the world's consumption of modern medicines, and it is the home of probably an even higher proportion of total "leading-edge" pharmaceutical R&D expenditure.

Such an analysis would be difficult in Europe, where national markets are highly fragmented, and the distribution of R&D investments among them is highly skewed. In the UK, the PPRS, which regulates industry profits from the NHS, has long been seen as the classic model, potentially linking returns to innovators with levels of national investment.

In a study of the Dutch medicines market, PriceWaterhouseCoopers (2004) developed a model which showed that, in Holland, a 1% decline in industry profits would lead to a 0.24% decline in R&D spending, in the short-term, and to a 0.4% decline in the long term. A US study concluded that government spending controls in Germany, Sweden, the UK, and France resulted in lower R&D spending by companies. It found that a decrease in drug prices by 1% led to a 0.7% drop in R&D spending (US General Accounting Office Report, 1994).

Abbott and Vernon (2005) used a micro-simulation model to analyse the response of R&D to changes in US prices. They found that large changes in price rapidly reduce investment incentives. Their study concludes:

> Most observers believe that the impact of our growing knowledge of the effects of genes and proteins will be the potential to develop highly targeted drugs for specific genotypes. The impact of this on the financial incentives for R&D could be dramatic; as the costs of development appear to be increasing and the potential market for each product seems to be shrinking. Thus, one might expect the prices of these newer, individualised medicines, to be extraordinarily high if they are to provide positive NPV projects at the initial "Go/No-go" decision point. Policies that put pressure on pharmaceutical prices could be expected to stifle such innovation.

Giaccotto *et al.* (2005) use an econometric model to identify a relationship between R&D and pricing for the period of 1952–2001. They demonstrated that a 1% decrease in the real average pharmaceutical price would lower R&D as a percentage of sales by 0.6%.

Golec *et al.* (2005) examined whether expected price constraints affect individual firms' R&D decisions. They concluded that expectations of price reductions reduce share prices and R&D expenditure.

Patent systems in OECD countries, which offer 20 years protection from imitators, provide the dominant incentive for pharmaceutical innovation. However, patents must be secured at the time of invention, and hence the intervening years needed for the development of innovations normally reduce the effective period of market protection to between ten and 12 years. As illustrated in Fig. 4, the achievement of a fair return is critically dependent upon both the patent life remaining at the time a product enters the market, and the revenue that can be generated across world markets in the years before the patent expires. After this time, revenues are almost completely lost to generic competitors.

The first in a new class that has a novel mechanism of action faces a major time-consuming challenge of changing established thinking and practice across the medical profession, world wide. However, while class follower NCEs are spared the initial pioneering work of selling a new treatment concept, they face the challenge of differentiating the product from the class leader and other closely related NMEs, in order to achieve sufficient market share to recover the R&D costs.

Pioneering studies of returns in the US over a 20-year period by Grabowski and Vernon (2000), show two important characteristics of pharmaceutical innovation:

1. A wide variance in the commercial success of NCEs launched into the market. Although a few products achieve very high rewards, many others did not even achieve sales that were sufficient enough to offset their R&D costs.
2. An uneven pattern in the correlation between the perceived healthcare added value and the rewards gained from individual products. In some cases, the first entrant in a radically innovative class was rapidly superseded by a "follow-on" drug, as happened when the anti-ulcer drug, Tagamet, was superseded by Zantac, a drug which was incrementally superior.

There appears to be a growing interest in models that classify new medicines into two discrete classes as a means of containing demand side healthcare costs: "breakthrough" drugs and "me-too" drugs (Morgan *et al.*, 2005). The essential aim of this approach is to reimburse all but a few perceived breakthroughs at low generic prices (Attridge and Sheridan, 2006). The substantial literature reviewed in this study indicates that such reimbursement policies of this type, which are now being applied more widely in Europe, are fundamentally incompatible with the *modus operandi* of the R&D based industry. They may also selectively damage new medium-sized, R&D-based European companies.

Epstein (2006) has recently drawn attention to the risk which over regulation poses to biopharmaceutical innovation in the US context.

In their Report for the European Commission, Pammolli *et al.* (2002) note that the contrast between the US experience and Europe's failure to generate competitive market structures has meant that innovative productivity in Europe is lagging further behind the US.

The growing scale of R&D expenditure has led to the development of more sophisticated models designed to optimise the allocation of expenditures across projects. Henderson and Cockburn (1996) drew attention to the positive correlation in the US between the productivity of R&D in the 1990s, and the intensive competition which is partly attributed to knowledge spillovers.

In the 1990s, the most significant constraint on industry appropriation of value has been the spread of cheap generics across world markets, which has reduced the area under the revenue curve in life cycle models (see Fig. 4). This process, which began in the US, has undoubtedly been a powerful driver of consolidation within the industry through merger and acquisition, which still continues even today. The upsurge in mergers and acquisitions reflects an increasing lack of confidence that R&D productivity can be restored, or that it can be compensated for by internal efficiency improvements across the business as a whole.

Within the R&D context, this trend reflects the uncertainties concerning whether the new bioscience wave of inventions can be translated fast enough into profitable innovations to sustain cash flows. In Europe, these uncertainties are compounded by the growing anxiety that multiple crises in healthcare funding will further constrain the funding of innovative treatments.

The Post-2000 Pharmaceutical Innovation Model

The dominant paradigm in the organisational development of the pharmaceutical industry in the second half of the 20th century was the evolution of the "big pharma", global "super tanker" model, which leveraged two core competences: the ability to do R&D in an increasingly efficient, integrated, "machine like" manner; and the "global marketing reach", designed to achieve effective diffusion. At the front end of the R&D process, external interfaces were often limited to a few universities at a national level. Similarly, although clinical trials must by definition be external, they are also often limited to national centres, as well as a few others in key world markets. Market approval dossier production and submissions were done on a sequential basis.

Major changes in this *modus operandi* occurred between 1990 and 2000, leading to the emergence of a post-2000 model, as illustrated in Fig. 6.

The key features of this model are:

1. A more complex pattern of international contractual relationships in the front end research phase, and a widespread belief that even "in-house" research units should be limited in size.
2. In research, signs that geographical clusters are giving way to open global research networks.
3. The pressure to speed up development through parallel processes and pragmatically outsourcing preclinical and clinical development have intensified, leading to more creative approaches to internationalising them to achieve greater efficiency.
4. Despite the substantial international harmonisation of regulatory requirements for market access, negotiating the content of dossiers and achieving actual approvals remains an unpredictable and high-risk process.
5. Outside of the USA, effective market entry requires diverse and often opaque forms of price negotiation and approval by state institutions or appointed surrogates. Particularly in Europe, downward cost containment pressure on prices has

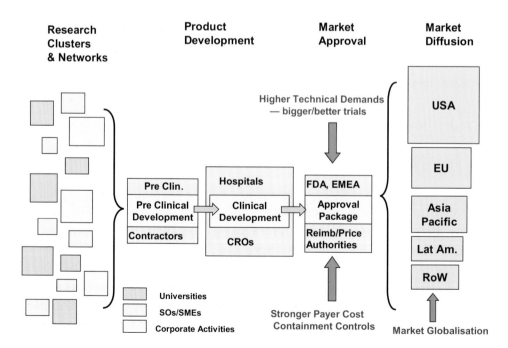

Fig. 6. The post-2000 model of pharma innovation.

increased. It appears likely to further reduce returns from numerous countries, especially new member states.

6. Greater efforts have been made to access a wider range of developed and middle-income countries (most notably, China and India) with R&D investment offered as a *quid pro quo.*

The final phase of the innovation process is achieving timely market diffusion of innovations to benefit both patients and the innovator. Expenditure on marketing by pharma companies has been commented on by critics who base their arguments upon a partial model of the innovation process which equates it to invention and R&D. This partial model fails to recognise that innovation is a cyclical, business driven process in which there will only be "repeat" innovation in the future if today's innovations complete the cycle through the market diffusion phase and generate revenues, which in part can be re-invested.

Conclusions

This review analyses the many models used for the bio-pharmaceutical sector in the wider context of general theories and models of innovation. It illustrates the complexities of a sector undergoing dramatic change both in its science and technology base and in the global markets for its products.

This study also addresses the underlying challenges in assessing the value of innovative products and the use of appropriate terminologies used for classifications. It raises serious doubts about how meaningful it is to make simple distinctions between "breakthrough" and "non-breakthrough" products, or even at the product level, the distinction between radical and incremental innovations. Research on the evolution of product classes over long time periods indicates that competitive development races and incremental differences seem to be the dominant paradigm.

Changes in the factors determining industry appropriation of value suggest that returns are diminishing on R&D outside of the US, which is likely to both constrain and narrow the scope of future investment. The short-term pressures that delay access to national markets and diffusion within markets at the beginning of the market life cycle, in conjunction with worldwide generic competition at the end, indicate that fewer new products will break even on development costs.

In the wider context of the bioscience wave, although there is a strong pattern of scientific advances and patentable inventions, it still remains in doubt whether closure can be brought to the innovative process through successful commercialisation.

There is a risk in Europe that the widespread social and economic benefits that have long been predicted from the biotechnology revolution could be either greatly diminished or substantially lost in the backwash of short-term healthcare cost containment. Building a better consensus on the models reviewed in this paper could help to reconcile the present widely differing views concerning how to achieve a balanced approach to effective budget control that would benefit payers, give patients rapid and open market access, and allow innovators to have prices that provide a fair financial return.

In particular this analysis would suggest:

1. A shift away from an emphasis on breakthrough products, towards a more balanced support for the dominant incremental innovation paradigm is needed, in conjunction with greater attention to facilitating the development and diffusion phases.
2. Cost containment measures by health purchasers which reduce prices and limit uptake of innovative products should be evaluated to assess their compatibility with the Lisbon agenda. A concerted effort is needed to audit existing regulations and identify and remove forms of regulation that discourage European investment in biopharmaceutical R&D.
3. New approaches are needed to regulation and "market-based" negotiation, based upon a more sophisticated appreciation of the nature of the innovation process. These new approaches will more effectively reconcile the needs of health-care systems to maintain budgetary discipline in the short term, while offering stronger incentives for European investment over the long term.

References

Abbott, TA and JA Vernon (2005). The cost of US pharmaceutical price reductions: a financial simulation model of R&D decisions. NBER Working Paper, pp. 1114–1118.

Abernathy WJ and JM Utterback (1975). A dynamic model of process and product innovation. *Omega*, 3, 6–12.

Achilladelis, B and N Antonakis (2001). The dynamics of technological innovation: the case of the pharmaceutical industry. *Research Policy*, 30, 535–542.

Adkins, S, I Smith and J Walton (2003). Lehman Brothers (1993–2003). *PharmaPipelines*, various issues.

AIM (2004). *i-Works: How High Value Innovation Networks can Boost UK Productivity*. London: ESRC/EPSRC Advanced Institute of Management Research.

Attridge, CJ (2006). Equity of access to innovative medicines: mission impossible? *IEA Economic Affairs*, September, 16–21.

Attridge, CJ and D Sheridan (2006). The impact of therapeutic reference pricing upon innovation in cardiovascular medicine. *Pharmacoeconomics*, 24(Suppl. 2).

Audretsch, DB, T Aldridge and A Oettl (2006). The knowledge filter and economic growth – the role of scientific entrepreneurship. Preliminary draft for the Ewing Kauffman Foundation.

Bailey, S, J Freeman and R Hybels (1994). Strategic alliances in commercial biotechnology. In *Networks and Organisations: Structure, Form and Action*, N Nohria and R Eades (eds.). Boston: HBS Press.

Baumol WJ (2002). *The Free Market Innovation Machine*. Princeton University Press.

Baumol, WJ (2006). Return of the invisible men: the microeconomic value theory of inventors and entrepreneurs. Paper presented at the American Economic Association Annual Meeting, 6–8 January. Available at URL: www.aeaweb.org/annual_mtg_papers/2006papers.html.

Berkhout, F and K Green (2003). Managing innovation for sustainability. *International Journal of Innovation Management*, 6(3).

Berndt, E (2003). Comparing diffusion paths of new pharmaceuticals in Canada and the USA. Paper Presented at iHEA 4th World Congress, San Francisco, (A) USA, 15–18 June.

Bhide, A (2006). Venturesome consumption, innovation and globalisation. CESIFO Conference on "Perspectives on the Performance of the Continent's Economies, Venice, 21–22 July. Available at URL: www.bhide.net/publications.html.

Boston Consulting Group (1999). *The Pharmaceutical Industry into Its Second Century: From Serendipity to Strategy.*

Bower, J (2003). Business model fashion and the academic spin out firm. *R&D Management* 33(2), 97–106.

Cambridge Pharma Consulting (2002). *Delays in Market Access*. Cambridge UK: Cambridge Pharma.

Cantwell, J (1992). The internationalisation of technological activity and its implications for competitiveness. In *Technology Management and International Business*, O Granstrand, L Hakanson and S Sjolander (eds.), pp. 75–95. Chichester: John Wiley.

Charles River Associates (2004). Innovation in the Pharmaceutical Sector: A Study Undertaken for the European Commission. *Available at http://*pharmacos.eudra.org/F2/pharmacos/docs/Doc2004/nov.

Chesborough, H (2003). *Open Innovation: The New Imperative for Creating and Profiting form Technology*. Boston, MA: Harvard Business School Press.

Comanor, WS (1986). The political economy of the pharmaceutical industry. *Journal of Economic Literature*, XXIV, 1178.

Conway, S and F Steward (2006). *Managing Innovation*. Oxford: Oxford University Press.

Daily Telegraph (2006). Venture Capital-Don't mind the gap, "it's a perception", Tuesday, 1 August, p. B8. Available at URL: www.telegraph.co.uk.

Danzon, PM and JD Kim (2002). *The Life Cycle of Pharmaceuticals: A Cross-national Perspective*. London: Office of Health Economics Monograph (OHE).

Deeds, DL, D DeCarolis and J Coombs (2000). Dynamic capabilities and new product development in high technology ventures: an empirical analysis of new biotechnology firms. *Journal of Business Venturing*, 15(3), 211–229.

Dickenson, ML and JW Gentry (1983). Characteristics of adopters and non-adopters of home computers. *Journal of Consumer Research*, 225.

DiMasi JA, RW Hansen, HG Grabowski and L Lasagna (1995). Research and development costs for new drugs by therapeutic category. *Pharmacoeconomics*, 7, 152.

DiMasi *et al.* (xxxx). *Clinical Development Times for New Drugs Drop 18% Reversing 12 Year Trend, July, Boston.* Boston, USA: Tufts Center for the Study of Drug Development.

Dosi, G, C Freeman, R Nelson, G Silverberg and L Soete (1988). *Technical Change and Economic Theory.* London: Francis Pinter.

Dosi, G (1982). Technological paradigms and technological trajectories. *Research Policy*, 11, 147–162.

Dosi G (1992). Research on innovation diffusion in economics of innovation — the case of the pharmaceutical industry. *Rivista Internazionale di Scienze Sociali*, 3, 219–228.

Epstein RA (2006). *Overdose: How Excessive Government Regulation Stifles Pharmaceutical Innovation.* Princeton, NJ, USA: Yale University Press.

Ernst and Young (2000) *European Life Sciences 2000.* London: Evolution.

Europe Economics (1998). Access to important new medicines; where and why do patients wait? See http://www.eer.co.uk.

Freeman, C (1982). *The Economics of Industrial Innovation.* London: Frances Pinter.

George, G, SA Zahra and D Robley-Wood (2002). The effects of business-university alliances on innovative output and financial performance: a study of publicly traded biotechnology companies. *Journal of Business Venturing*, 17, 577–609.

Giaccotto, C, RE Santerre and JA Vernon (2005). Pharmaceutical pricing and R&D growth rates. *Journal of Law and Economics*, 48, 195–214.

Golec, J, S Hedge and JA Vernon (2005). Pharmaceutical stock reactions to price constraint threats and firm-level R&D spending. NBER Working Paper 11229.

Grabowski, H and J Vernon (2000). The distribution of sales revenues from pharmaceutical innovation. *Pharmacoeconomics*, 18(Suppl. 1), 21.

Griffin, J (1985). *Therapeutic Conservatism in UK Medicine.* London: ABPI.

Haigh, J (2004). *Developing an Indicator for Market Access Delays in Europe.* IMS Global Consulting at http.//www.imshealth.com.

Henderson, RM and IM Cockburn (1996). Scale Scope and spillovers: determinants of research productivity in the pharmaceutical industry. *RAND Journal of Economics*, 27, 32.

von Hippel, E (1986). Lead users: a source of novel product concepts. *Management Science*, 32.

von Hippel, E (1976). Users as innovators. *Technology Review*, 5, 212.

Jonsson, B and N Wilking (2005). *A pan-European Comparison Regarding Patient Access to Cancer Drugs.* Stockholm: Karolinska Institutet and Department of Economics, Stockholm University.

Kettler, HE (1998). *Competition through Innovation, Innovation through Competition.* London: Office of Health Economics, Monograph.

Kettler, HE and S Casper (2000). *The Road to Sustainability in the UK and German Biotechnology* Industries. London: Office of Health Economics, Monograph.

Kings Fund (2006). *Local Variations in NHS Spending Priorities — Briefing Paper*, August, at http://www.kingsfund.org.uk.

Landau, R, D Achilladelis and A Scriabine (1999). *Pharmaceutical Innovation — Revolutionising Human Health*. Philadelphia, USA: Chemical Heritage Press.

Laursen, K (1997). Horizontal diversification in the Danish national system of innovation: the case of pharmaceuticals. *Research Policy*, 25, 1121.

Lerner, J and R Meyers (1998). The control of technology alliances: an empirical analysis of the biotechnology industry. *The Journal of Industrial Economics*, XLVI, 125.

Levin, RC, AK Klevonick, RR Nelson and SG Winter (1987). Appropriating the returns from industrial R&D. *Brookings Papers on Economic Activity*, 3, 794.

Lichtenberg, FR (2005). Pharmaceutical knowledge-capital accumulation and longevity. In *Measuring Capital in the New Economy*, C Corrado, J Haltiwanger and D Sichrl (eds.). Chicago, USA: University of Chicago.

Mansfield, E (1986). Patents and innovation: an empirical study. *Management Science*, 175.

Mansfield, E (1989). The diffusion of industrial robots in Japan and the US, *Research Policy*, 15, 193.

McKelvey, M, H Alm and M Riccaboni (2003). Does co-location matter for formal knowledge collaboration in the Swedish biotechnology–pharmaceutical sector? *Research Policy*, 32, 483.

Morgan, SG, KL Bassett, JM Wright, RG Evans, ML Barer, PL Caetano and CD Black (2005). Breakthrough drugs and growth in expenditure on prescription drugs in Canada. *British Medical Journal*, 331, 815–816.

Mowbery, DC and N Rosenberg (1979). The influence of market demand on innovation: a critical review of some recent empirical studies. *Research Policy*, 8(1).

Mueller, DC (1986). *Profits in the Long Run*, pp. 11–42. Cambridge, UK: Cambridge University Press.

Myers, S (1999). Measuring pharmaceutical risk and the cost of capital. In *Risk and Return in the Pharmaceutical Industry*, J Sussex and N Marchant (eds.). London: OHE.

Nelson, R (ed.) (1993). *National Innovation Systems*. Oxford: Oxford University Press.

Nelson, RR and SG Winter (1982). *An Evolutionary Theory of Economic Change*. Cambridge, MA: Bellnap Press.

Nelson, RR and SG Winter (1997). In search of a useful theory of innovation. *Research Policy*, 6(36).

Nicholls-Nixon, CL and CY Woo (2003). Technology souring and the output of established firms in a regime encompassing technological change. *Strategic Management Journal*, 24, 651–666.

Nightingale, P and P Martin (2004). The myth of the biotech revolution. *Trends in Biotechnology*, 22, 564.

OECD (2006). *Innovation in Pharmaceutical Biotechnology: Comparing National Innovation Systems at the Sectoral Level*. Paris, France: OECD. Available at URL: www.oecd.org/sti/innovation.

Orsenigo, L, F Pammolli and M Riccaboni (2001). Technological change and network dynamics: lessons from the pharmaceutical industry. *Research Policy*, 30, 485–508.

Pammolli, F, L Orsenigo, M Riccaboni, M Mariani, A Gambardella, A Bonaccorsai and A Allansdottir (2002). *Innovation and Competitiveness in European Biotechnology.* Enterprise Paper No. 7. Brussels: Enterprise Directorate-General, European Commission. Available at URL: www.europa.eu.int.

Pammolli, F, M Riccaboni and L Magazzini (2003). The dynamics of competition in pharmaceuticals: on patent expiry, generic penetration and industry structure. *4th iHEA World Congress*, San Francisco, USA, 15–18 June.

Parker, JES (1984). *The International Diffusion of Pharmaceuticals.* New York: St Martins Press.

Patel, P (1995). The localised production of global technology. *Cambridge Journal of Economics*, 19, 141–153.

Patel, P and K Pavitt (1994). National innovation systems: why they are important, and how they might be measured and compared. *Economics of Innovation and New Technology*, 3, 77–95.

Pavitt, K (1990). What we know about the strategic management of technology. *California Management Review*, 32(3).

Payer, L (1989). *Medicine and Culture — Notions of Health and Sickness in Britain, the US, France and West Germany.* London: Victor Gollanz Ltd.

Perez, C (1985). Microelectronics, long waves and world structural change. *World Development*, 13, 441.

Pisano, GP (2006). *Science Business: The Promise, the Reality and the Future of Biotech.* Cambridge, MA, USA: Harvard Business School Press.

Porter, M (1990). *The Competitive Advantage of Nations.* London: Macmillan.

PriceWaterhouseCoopers (2004). Economische analyse van het 'Plan Hoogervorst'.' Eindrapport 02 18, p. 64.

Robb R (2006). Europes venture capital institutions are good enough. Paper presented at CESIFO Conference on 'Perspectives on the performance of the continents' economies. San Servolo, Venice, 21–22 July.

Rogers, EM (1962). *Diffusion of Innovations.* New York: Free Press.

Rothearmel, FT (2001).Complementary assets, strategic alliances and the incumbents advantage: an empirical study of industry and firm effects in the biopharmaceutical industry. *Research Policy*, 30, 1235–1251.

Rothearmel, FT and DL Deeds (2004). Exploration and exploitation alliances in biotechnology: a system of new product development. *Strategic Management Journal*, 25, 201–221.

Rothwell, R (1992a). Successful industrial innovation; critical factors for the 1990's. *R&D Management*, 22, 221.

Rothwell, R (1992). Industrial innovation and government regulation. *Technovation*, 12, 447.

Rothwell, R (1984). The role of small firms in the emergence of new technologies. *Omega*, 12, 19.

Schmidt, GM (2004). Low-end and high-end encroachments for new products. *International Journal of Innovation Management*, 8(2), 167–192.

Scherer, FM (2004). The pharmaceutical industry — prices and progress. *New England Journal of Medicine*, 351(9), 927–932.

Schmookler, J (1966). *Invention and Economic Growth*. Harvard University Press.

Schumpeter, JA (1934). *The Theory of Economic Development*. Harvard University Press.

Schumpeter, JA (1963). *Capitalism, Socialism and Democracy*. New York: Harper & Low.

Schumpeter, JA (1939). *Business Cycles*. New York: McGraw Hill.

Schoffski, O (2002). *Diffusion of Medicines in Europe*. Burgdorf, Germany: Health Economics Research Centre.

Schweitzer, SO (1997). *Pharmaceutical Economics and Policy*. Oxford: Oxford University Press.

Sharp, ML (1999). Pharmaceuticals and biotechnology. In *Perspectives for the European Industry in Technology*, C Freeman, M Sharp and W Walker (eds.).

Sharp, ML (1999). The science of nations: European multinationals and American biotechnology. *International Journal of Biotechnology*, 1, 132.

Stalk, G (1988). Time — the next source of competitive advantage. *Harvard Business Review*, July, 41.

Thomas, L (1994). Implicit industrial policy: the triumph of Britain and the failure of France in global pharmaceuticals. *Industrial and Corporate Change*, 3, 451–489.

Tidd J (2006). *Innovation Models, Discussion Paper*. London: Tanaka Business School, Imperial College.

Tidd, J, J Bessant and K Pavitt (2005). *Managing Innovation: Integrating Technological, Market and Organizational Change*, 3rd Edn. Wiley.

Tushman, M and P Anderson (1987). Technological discontinuities and organizational environments. *Administrative Science Quarterly*, 31(3), 439–465.

US General Accounting Office Report (1994). Prescription drugs: spending controls in four European countries. GAO/HEHS-94-30.

Utterback, J (1994). *Mastering the Dynamics of Innovation*, p. 256. Boston, MA: Harvard Business School Press.

Utterback, J and HJ Acee (2005). Disruptive technologies: an expanded view. *International Journal of Innovation Management*, 9(1), 1–18.

Walley, T, P Folino-Gallo, U Schwabe and E van Ganse (2004). Variations and increase in the use of statins in Europe: data from administrative databases. *British Medical Journal*, 328, 385–386.

Wells, N (1988). *Innovative Chemical Extensions — The Economic Basis of Pharmaceutical Progress*. London: OHE (Monograph).

Zucker, LG and MR Darby (1997). Present at the biotechnological revolution: transformation of technological identity for a large incumbent pharmaceutical firm. *Research Policy*, 26, 429.

DEVELOPMENT AND INNOVATION IN CARDIOVASCULAR MEDICINE

DESMOND SHERIDAN

Department of Cardiology
National Heart and Lung Institute Imperial College London
St Mary's Hospital, Norfolk Place
W2 1PG London, UK
d.sheridan@imperial.ac.uk

The last century has witnessed groundbreaking advances in clinical medicine across the entire diagnostic and therapeutic range, but inequities in access to these advances and innovations continue to be a major challenge to our societies.

Innovations are often initiated by "eureka" moments of discovery, but realising their full potential depend on a process of continuous incremental innovation and interaction involving complex networks. When developing systems that reward, encourage, and sustain medical advances, policy makers must recognise four important factors. First, "incremental" and "continuous" innovation is as important as "breakthrough" innovation. Second, investment across the entire innovation process is needed. Third, the ability of physicians to work across a wide range of scientific fields at "the bench and bedside" is critical to continuous innovation. And fourth, final medical advance that can result from an initial discovery may not be obvious and only occur following interaction with experts and innovations in other fields.

Keywords: Innovation; incremental; eureka; cardiovascular; diagnostics; therapeutics.

Introduction

The past century has seen dramatic advances in clinical medicine across the entire diagnostic and therapeutic range. In the last decades most developed countries have enjoyed a substantial reduction in mortality from cardiovascular disease. These achievements have resulted from (1) a better understanding of cardiovascular disease, (2) developments and innovations in diagnostic methods, and (3) new drugs, technologies and surgical methods.

As impressive as past successes have been, the need for future advances is of equal measure. Despite an approximate 50% reduction in deaths from coronary heart disease in recent decades in most developed countries, it will remain the greatest cause of mortality and morbidity on a global scale in the decades ahead. The growing burden of cardiovascular disease linked to obesity and diabetes is the new and emerging challenge to cardiovascular science.

The rapid advances in science that led to new drugs and technologies have also created a significant challenge to healthcare providers in delivering effective care for patients: increased demand for more effective and more widely available medicines will continue to challenge biomedical science in the future. Should further scientific advances be considered "a burden" on the health delivery process? Should we seek to curtail further advances and focus on control of healthcare costs, or should we encourage future advances, confident that success will bring health and economic benefits?

How will biomedical science rise to these challenges? In considering this, an understanding of the way advances have been made in the past and the challenges ahead is important. This paper will outline some of the major developments that have emerged over the past century and challenges for the future, using cardiovascular medicine as an example.

Early Developments

Harvey's understanding of the circulation of the blood was based on detailed anatomical studies and was a key breakthrough of the Enlightenment. Understanding circulatory function *in vivo*, particularly in man, has always been a challenge due to its relative inaccessibility. The early physicians developed remarkable clinical skills for examining the heart and circulation based on close observation, aided by the stethoscope introduced by Laennec in 1816, the first great technical development in cardiovascular medicine. The first modern breakthrough for the assessment of cardiac function was the electrocardiogram (ECG). First recorded in man by Waller (1887), Einthoven (1895) later established the power of the ECG to reveal important aspects of cardiac function. The contributions by Waller and Einthoven are classic examples of "development" and "innovation" applied to medicine. Waller demonstrated and published the principle using a mercury capillary electrometer; Einthoven applied the much more sensitive string galvanometer to collect recordings of better quality. This innovation opened the way for a wide range of techniques for diagnosing abnormalities in the heart rhythm as well as its structure and function.

Coronary heart disease is the most frequent cause of death in the developed world (Murray and Lopez, 1997) and the ECG remains the most widely used technique for diagnosing it. During the 20th century innovations of the basic ECG have spawned a wide range of new techniques and treatments. For example, the ability to record the ECG from within the cardiac chambers using flexible electrodes introduced percutaneously in conscious patients led to the development of techniques for the detailed study of cardiac dysrhythmias (Denes *et al.*, 1973). This in turn was instrumental in the application of radio frequency ablation therapy for the permanent cure of many forms of dysrhythmia (Kay *et al.*, 1992). Similarly, it was ECG analysis of rhythm abnormalities that led to the concept and introduction of cardiac pacing (Bigelow *et al.*, 1950) for bradydysrhythmias and of defibrillation for ventricular fibrillation (Beck *et al.*, 1947). Thus, a discovery originally based on the use of a simple capillary electrometer has with successive innovations become the bedrock for the clinical investigation of almost all forms of heart disease. Waller initially did not imagine that "electrocardiography would play any very extensive use in the hospital" and only with further research and innovation came to realise the full potential of his initial recordings.

Cardiovascular Imaging

Ultrasound imaging

While the ECG provides indirect information about cardiac function based on its electrical activity, direct imaging of the heart adds great diagnostic potential. Echocardiography utilises the fact that high-frequency sound waves travel safely through tissues at a known velocity and are reflected by tissue boundaries of differing acoustic density. In practice, a piezoelectric crystal is used to generate high-frequency sound waves and to detect "echoes" from reflecting surfaces. Time and frequency analysis of reflected ultrasound provides valuable information about the structure and function of the cardiac chambers and valves (Keidel, 1950). From this initial invention a host of innovations have followed. Examples of this have been the introduction of phased array or rocking transducers, creating a fan-shaped imaging field that results in a two-dimensional anatomical view of the heart in any chosen plane. This advance greatly improved diagnostic power (Edler and Hertz, 1954), providing valuable diagnostic information about cardiac chamber size and contractile function. A further refinement was the analysis of frequency shifts in the reflected ultrasound which provides information about blood flow velocity and direction within the heart and blood vessels (Feigenbaum *et al.*, 2004). Colour coding of displayed images based on the frequency shift of reflected sound allows the direction and velocity of blood flow to be displayed. Valvular motion and orifice areas can be determined and estimates of blood pressure gradients across valves can also be derived. Complex congenital heart diseases including intra-cardiac shunts can be examined. In addition, by using transducers with different depths of view, these techniques can be applied to the study of blood vessels at different depths within the body. More recently, intravascular ultrasound methods have been developed using transducers mounted on the end of flexible catheters that can be inserted percutaneously into coronary arteries to assess disease prior to and following intervention (Tobis *et al.*, 1989). Thus, we again see a remarkable diagnostic invention that reaches its full potential through several innovations and refinements.

X-ray imaging

Coronary heart disease has been the greatest challenge to cardiovascular medicine. Successes in preventing and treating this disease have contributed most to the reduction in cardiovascular disease mortality. Long-term prognosis in individual patients is related to the extent of atheromatous deposits within the coronary arteries (Mock *et al.*, 1982). Imaging of coronary arteries is beyond the resolution of current ultrasound techniques, and still relies on an innovation of one of the earliest imaging techniques, X-rays. Coronary angiography involves the introduction of a flexible catheter through a small skin puncture, which can be advanced to the orifice of the coronary arteries. Transient injections of contrast media allow visualisation of the vessel lumen during X-ray examination.

The introduction of coronary angiography is a typical example of the incremental nature of medical advances and of the combination of serendipity and vision that often underpins it. During a routine cardiac catheterisation, when aortography was done to assess the patency of the aortic valve, the catheter inadvertently slipped into the right coronary ostium, and a selective coronary angiogram was performed (Hurst, 1985). This unexpected event led to the introduction of routine diagnostic coronary angiography. The basic principles of angiography are unchanged, but several refinements and innovations have enhanced its image quality and ease of use. Initially recorded on cine film and later on videotape, modern systems rely on digital storage coupled with image enhancement. Together, these innovations provide images of much better quality and with greatly reduced exposure of patients and operators to radiation. Coronary stenoses (narrowings) can be assessed in terms of their severity, distribution, and number, providing accurate prognostic information and an essential guide to treatment. In this way, innovations that improved the efficiency, diagnostic power, and safety of angiography have led to its routine use, and underpinned the widespread introduction of coronary artery bypass surgery (Ryan, 2002). The development of coronary angioplasty and stenting can also be traced through an innovative line from the technique of angiography. Catheters used for angiography have undergone multi-step innovative developments in their design fabrication and construction. One innovation in catheter design involved mounting an inflatable balloon close to the catheter tip, which could be deployed within coronary arteries to dilate a stenosis (Gruentzig *et al.*, 1979). Angioplasty was soon demonstrated to be more effective than medical therapy in controlling symptoms of angina pectoris (Strauss *et al.*, 1995) and was rapidly established in routine clinical practice. The phenomenon of re-stenosis in the first three months following angioplasty led to further intensive research, and ultimately to the development of intra-coronary stents. These consist of tiny metal cylinders in which multiple "cuts" had been placed, such that when stretched over an inflated angioplasty balloon, they stent the dilated artery. Early bare metal stents were successful in reducing re-stenosis but not in preventing it entirely (Serruys *et al.*, 1994). The most recent innovation has been to cover stents with a biodegradable material containing drugs that inhibit re-stenosis. Gradual local release is achieved, and this further reduces the risk of re-stenosis. Known as drug-eluting stents, they represent the most recent innovation of the technique. Early studies suggest a substantial further reduction in the rate of re stenosis (Morice *et al.*, 2002).

Thus, the evolution of coronary angiography and intervention has been a remarkable collaboration between physicians, clinical scientists, engineers and technologists. It is also an example of where the initial invention has undergone profound change and development through repeated innovation that was driven by the challenge to meet a major unmet clinical need, and a confidence in the ability to do so.

Development and Innovation in Cardiovascular Therapies

Several drugs in regular use today were introduced prior to the development of modern pharmacology. Digoxin, a glycoside from the foxglove digitalis purpurea, was used as a plant extract for many decades. Aspirin was first extracted from willow as salicin in 1825 and introduced in synthetic form in 1874. Thomas Lauder Brunton demonstrated the anti-anginal properties of amyl nitrate in the early 19th century, long before the cause of this condition was understood. Modern developments in cardiovascular pharmacology originate in our understanding of receptor pharmacology.

β-blockers

The discovery of adrenergic receptors (Ahlquist, 1948)and their role in autonomic regulation of cardiovascular function led to the discovery of receptor antagonists. *β*-Blockers, discovered by Sir James Black (Black *et al.*, 1965), have a well-established place in the modern therapy of angina pectoris, hypertension and cardiac failure. The benefits of *β*-blockade all relate to antagonism of *β*-adrenergic stimulation, as do most of the adverse effects associated with *β*-blockers. Successful widespread use of *β*-blockers required a detailed understanding of pharmacological effects mediated by *β*-adrenergic receptor subtypes (Lands *et al.*, 1967), and on innovations in drug design to achieve selective receptor antagonism. The most serious adverse effects of β-blockers are caused by blockade of β-2 mediated bronchodilatation, vasodilatation, and mobilisation of glucose and free fatty acids. The introduction of β-1 selective antagonists substantially reduced the risk of these side-effects (Rolf Smith *et al.*, 1983; Head *et al.*, 1995), whereas β-2 specific agonists have proved successful in treating asthma (Svedmyr, 1985). It is remarkable that approximately two decades after the introduction of β-blockers, chronically elevated β-adrenergic activity was discovered to be one of several important neurohumoral disturbances associated with an adverse prognosis in heart failure (Mark, 1995). This in turn led to studies of β-blockers in heart failure which showed a significant benefit to survival (CIBIS Investigators and Committees, 1999). Thus, β-blocking drugs possess a range of properties depending on their receptor specificity and molecular characteristics. Developments in understanding receptor characteristics and innovations in drug design, following the initial introduction of this class of drugs, have substantially improved our ability to use these drugs to maximum benefit.

Calcium antagonists

It has been known since the late 19th century (Ringer, 1887) that calcium ions play a critical role in the contraction of cardiac muscle. A similar role in smooth muscle contraction was demonstrated later. Flekenstein (Byon and Fleckenstein, 1969) showed in 1968 that Verapamil has properties on cardiac muscle similar to withdrawal of calcium ions. He later went on to demonstrate that its action was due to a decoupling of the electromechanical process, and was specifically related to antagonism of a calcium-specific action. These studies led to the introduction of a new class of drugs; the calcium antagonists of which the prototype, Verapamil, remains in use for the treatment of supraventricular dysrhythmias, angina pectoris and hypertension. However, following the discovery of Verapamil it was soon learned that its actions applied both to cardiac and to smooth muscle, and that the availability of calcium antagonists with greater tissue specificity would be beneficial. Calcium antagonists acting on cardiac muscle cause a negative inotropic effect (Joshi *et al.*, 1981) and slow conduction through the atrioventricular node (Rinkenberger *et al.*, 1980); whereas those acting on smooth muscle cause vasodilatation. This understanding led the development of calcium antagonist drugs with greater tissue specificity for cardiac or smooth muscle, and consequently to more precise pharmacological action. In current practice, calcium antagonists acting on smooth muscle are most widely used to treat hypertension. In contrast, for the treatment of supraventricular dysrhythmias, cardiac-acting drugs such as Verapamil are needed. The calcium antagonists are therefore a drug class, which was initially developed on the basis of an understanding of electro mechanical coupling in muscular tissues, and which has evolved as a result of innovations based on an understanding of tissue-specific structure–functional relationships. In addition, as is so often the case, the drug most widely used in clinical practice today is a refinement of the initial prototype; a result of innovations leading to more specific action and more favourable pharmacodynamics.

ACE inhibitors

The renin angiotensin aldosterone system (RAAS) is a powerful regulator of the circulation. Angiotensin II, formed from angiotensin I by the action of the angiotensin-converting enzyme (ACE), is a potent vasoconstrictor. It enhances adrenergic stimulation and causes the release of aldosterone (Kang *et al.*, 1994). Inhibition of ACE was recognised as a potentially important therapeutic target, and a large series of ACE inhibitors have been developed. ACE inhibitors have been shown to be effective antihypertensive agents with particular benefits for diabetic patients. They have also been shown to reduce mortality in patients with chronic heart failure (CONSENSUS Trial Study Group, 1987), a substantial therapeutic breakthrough since prognosis in heart failure is similar to many forms of cancer and is resistant to treatment. The vascular complications of type II diabetes and metabolic syndrome are some of the greatest therapeutic challenges for cardiovascular medicine. Clinical trials showing that ACE inhibition confers cardiovascular protection in diabetes are important, not only in establishing new therapies, but also in pointing the way towards a better understanding of this complex syndrome.

At present, classification of ACE inhibitors is based on pharmacokinetic characteristics. Class 1 consists of captopril-like compounds that are already active, but are metabolised by the liver into products, some of which also have pharmacological activity, and all of which are excreted by the kidney. Class 2, the largest series, are pro-drugs converted to active forms in the liver. Class 3 are water-soluble active molecules which are excreted in the urine unchanged. Two potentially troublesome side-effects of ACE inhibitors are persistent cough and angio-oedema. The precise mechanisms responsible for these adverse effects are not clear. However, accumulation of endogenous vasodilator substances such as bradykinin is a possible mediator (Ferner *et al.*, 1987), since the ACE is also responsible for their catabolism. In terms of innovation and development, the ACE inhibitors might not yet be fully evolved. They have made a profound impact on the treatment of hypertension, particularly in diabetic subjects (Yusef *et al.*, 2000), in reducing mortality due to chronic heart failure (CONSENSUS Trial Study Group, 1987),and in preserving left ventricular function following myocardial infarction. However, the full complexity of the role of the RAAS and bradykinin systems in vascular pathology remains to be fully elucidated. Therapeutic advances to date indicate that this system is likely to have a powerful role in mediating the complex interactions between abnormal glucose metabolism and vascular pathology. Therefore it will remain the focus of intense research. As the picture becomes clarified, opportunities for further innovation of ACE inhibitors and other modulation of the RAAS and bradykinin system will emerge.

Antithrombotic therapy

Angina pectoris was first described by Heberden in 1768. Parry attributed it to coronary artery disease in 1799. However it was not until the early 20th century that this was widely accepted. For example, in 1923, McKenzie published a book on angina pectoris in which he attributed the condition to heart failure. One of the most important achievements of the second half of the 20th century was the development of a more detailed understanding of the pathology of acute and chronic coronary atheromatous disease. In particular, understanding of the importance of coronary plaque and plaque instability, along with the importance of endothelial integrity in maintaining blood flow and prevention of thrombosis, have been critical. Experimental studies undoubtedly contributed to this, but the intensive study of patients in the early stages of myocardial infarction that was made possible following the introduction of coronary care units was extremely important (Julian, 2001). In addition, the introduction of coronary angiography permitted the recognition of coronary angiographic features associated with unstable coronary syndromes. Understanding that thrombosis was a key element in precipitating heart attacks led to the introduction of thrombolytic treatment (Rentrop et al., 1979). Streptokinase, which was discovered in 1933 following the observation that an infiltrate of a culture of group C streptococci could lyse human plasma clot (Tillet and Garner, 1933), was first successfully used to liquefy pleural clot (Tillet and Sherry, 1949). Early studies in acute myocardial infarction gave conflicting, but overall encouraging results, which justified large randomised clinical trials that eventually demonstrated the ability of thrombolytic treatment to reduce mortality, and to preserve myocardial function when given early to patients with evolving heart attacks (Italian Group for the Study of Strptokinase in Myocardial Infarction (GISSI), 1986).

Although originally extracted from willow in 1825, the mechanisms of the anti-platelet properties of aspirin were not discovered until 1971 (Ferreira et al., 1971). Platelet micro-embolisation had been demonstrated at post-mortem examination in the coronary arteries of victims of sudden cardiac death. This led to the concept that the anti-platelet properties of aspirin may be beneficial in preventing complications of coronary heart disease. The ISIS-2 study (ISIS-2 Collaboration Group, 1988), demonstrated the ability of aspirin to reduce mortality in patients suffering from heart attacks. Both aspirin and streptokinase had been available for approximately 150 and 50 years, respectively, prior to these discoveries. Their "rediscovery" as successful treatments for coronary disease is an excellent example of the value of ongoing research and innovation to make better use of existing drugs. In relation to thrombolytic therapy, the key developments that allowed their widespread and rapid use were (1) the introduction highly successful large (mega) clinical trails, (2) evidence that their efficacy did not require intra-coronary delivery, and (3) recognition that optimal effectiveness was critically dependent on their use as soon as possible after the onset of the symptoms of myocardial infarction.

Lipid lowering drugs

It has been known for several decades that plasma cholesterol level is a major risk factor for coronary heart disease. For most of that period, this knowledge was coupled with uncertainty as to whether lowering cholesterol levels would confer any benefit in preventing complications of coronary heart disease. Treatments had been available to lower plasma lipids, and had been shown to reduce the complications of coronary heart disease but not overall mortality (Co-operative trial in the primary prevention of ischaemic heart disease using clofibrate, 1978). The key development which advanced lipid-lowering therapy was understanding lipid transport (Brown and Goldstein, 1976), which in turn, led to the breakthrough introduction of statins, which block cholesterol synthesis in the liver by inhibiting the enzyme 3-hydroxy-3-methylglutaryl coenzyme-A reductase. In a landmark study, the "4-S" trial clearly demonstrated a reduction in overall mortality in patients who had a previous history of angina or myocardial infarction and who were given statin therapy for 5 years (Scandinavian Simvastatin Survival Study Group, 1994). This led to the widespread introduction of statins for the prevention of complications in patients with coronary heart disease. Important questions remained as to the use of statins in other patient groups — for example, in patients with cerebral vascular disease, peripheral vascular disease, and diabetes. These have now been the subject of major clinical trials. The Heart Protection Study Collaborative Group (2002), which investigated over 25,000 patients with peripheral vascular disease, clearly showed survival benefit in patients with peripheral vascular disease and cerebral vascular disease, including a reduction in stroke and overall mortality. A large sub-study of the ASCOT trial (Sever *et al.*, 2003) subsequently demonstrated that patients who are being treated for hypertension derive additional benefit when given statin therapy. More recently, the CARDS trial (Colhoun *et al.*, 2004) has demonstrated that patients with type II diabetes have significantly improved survival when given statin therapy. These clinical trials exemplify the concept that a drug is only as good as our understanding of how to use it effectively to benefit patients. It is essential to recognise the innovative importance and value of studies that extend our understanding of how to use drugs more effectively.

Therapeutic advances arise in a number of ways. They result from (1) innovation and refinement in drug design to achieve better structure-functional relationships. However, they also result from (2) a better understanding of how to use drugs, and defining the patient groups that will benefit from them. There is a tendency to regard the second as being of less fundamental value and that the information they provide can be generally applied to the entire class of drugs. This however, is not the case, since benefit may be related to particular pharmacokinetic or other characteristics of a particular formulation. Therefore it is important that research and development leading to new uses of existing drugs or innovative formulations of delivery systems should be encouraged and recognised for its value.

Conclusions

This historical review clearly shows that all major advances in cardiovascular medicine are built on a process of continuous innovation, which in many cases can be traced back to a technical development in a non-clinical or even non-medical field.

Clinical medicine shows a remarkable ability to harvest developments from outside its own area and apply them to solve diagnostic and therapeutic challenges.

The ability of physicians to work across a wide range of scientific fields at "the bench and bedside" has been an important aspect of this. This can be attributed to the traditionally strong place of science in the medical curriculum.

The final medical advance that can result from a discovery may not be obvious even to the scientists initially involved; they frequently depend on interaction with experts and innovations in other fields.

For most classes of drug therapy, the prototype agent is usually superseded by more effective, specific and safer follow-up developments.

Aspirin, streptokinase and β-blockers are excellent examples of drugs which benefit patients whose diseases were not considered for their use for years or even decades following their initial introduction. Innovations that lead to better use of existing drugs are as important as their initial discovery, and must be encouraged.

These issues have important implications in developing systems that reward, encourage and facilitate medical advances. Innovations are often initiated by "eureka" moments of discovery, but their full potential is almost always dependent on a process of continuous innovation and development through a complex network of interaction. This suggests that investment across the entire innovation process is needed to sustain developments in medicine. Targeting investment at particular areas of research, for example, in biotechnology will only be successful in leading to applicable advances if discoveries can be taken forward through an established clinical, non-clinical and industrial network.

References

Ahlquist, RP (1948). A study of adrenotropic receptors. *American Journal of Physiology*, 153, 586–600.

Beck, CS, WH Pritchard and SA Feil (1947). Ventricular fibrillation of long duration abolished by electric shock. *JAMA*, 135, 985–989.

Bigelow, WG, JC Callaghan and JA Hopps (1950). General hypothermia for experimental intracardiac surgery. *Annals of Surgery*, 1132, 531–539.

Black, JW, WA Duncan and RG Shanks (1965). Comparison of some properties of pronethalol and propranolol. *British Journal of Pharmacology Chemotherapy*, 25, 577–591.

Brown, MS and JL Goldstein (1976). Receptor mediated control of cholesterol metabolism. *Science*, 191, 150–154.

Byon, KY and A Fleckenstein (1969). Parallel influence of isometric tension development and O2 consumption of isolated papillary muscles under the influence of Ca ions, adrenaline, isoproteranol and organic Ca antagonists (iproveratril, D 600, prenylamine). *Pflugers Archic*, 312(1), R8–R9.

Colhoun, HM, DJ Betteridge, PN Durrington, GA Hitman, HAW Neil, SJ Livingstone, MJ Thomason, MI Mackness, V Charlton-Menys and JH Fuller. On behalf of the CARDS investigators (2004). Primary prevention of cardiovascular disease with atorvastatin in type 2 diabetes in the Collaborative Atorvastatin Diabetes Study (CARDS); multicentre randomized placebo-controlled trial. *Lancet*, 364, 685–696.

CIBIS Investigators and Committees (1999). The Cardiac Insufficiency Bisoprolol Study II (CIBIS-II); a randomized trial. *Lancet*, 353, 9–13.

CONSENSUS Trial Study Group (1987). Effects of enalapril on mortality in severe congestive heart failure. Results of the cooperative North Scandinavian Enalapril Survival Study (CONSENSUS). *The New England Journal of Medicine*, 316, 1429–1435.

Co-operative trial in the primary prevention of ischaemic heart disease using clofibrate (1978). Report from the committee of principal investigators. *British Heart Journal*, 40(10), 1069–1118.

Denes, P, D Wu, RC Dhingra, R Chuquimia and KM Rosen (1973). Demonstration of dual A-V nodal pathways in patients with paroxysmal supraventricular tachycardia. *Circulation*, 48, 549–555.

Einthoven, W (1895). Ueber die Form des menschlichen Electrocardiograms. *Arch f d Ges Physiol*, 60, 101–123.

Edler, I and CH Hertz (1954). The use of ultrasonic reflectoscope for the continuous recording of the movements of heart walls. *Kungl Fysiografiska sallskapets i Lund forhandlingar*, 24(5), 1–19.

Feigenbaum, H, WF Armstrong and T Ryan (2004). *Echocardiography*. Philadelphia.

Ferner, RE, JM Simpson and MD Rawlins (1987). Effects of intradermal bradykinin after inhibition of angiotensin converting enzyme. *British Medical Journal*, 294, 1119–1120.

Ferreira, SH, S, Moncada and JR Vane (1971). Indomethicin and aspirin abolish prostaglandin release from the spleen. *Nature New Biology*, 231, 237–239.

Gruentzig, AR, A Seining and WE Seigenthaler (1979). Non-operative dilatation of coronary artery stenosis in percutaneous transluminal coronary angioplasty. *The New England Journal of Medicine*, 301, 61–68.

Head, A, MJ Kendall and S Maxwell (1995). Exercise metabolism during 1 hour of treadmill walking while taking high and low doses of propranolol, metoprolol or placebo. *Clinical Cardiology*, 18, 335–340.

Heart Protection Study Collaborative Group (2002). MRC/BHF Heart Protection Study of cholesterol lowering with simvastatin in 20 536 high risk individuals: a randomized placebo controlled trial. *Lancet*, 306, 7–22.

Hurst, JW (1985). History of cardiac catheterisation. In SB King III and JS Douglas (eds.), pp. 1–9. McGraw-Hill.

ISIS-2 (Second International Study of Infarct Survival) Collaboration Group (1988). Randomised trial of intravenous streptokinase, oral aspirin, both or neither among cases of suspected acute myocardial infarction: ISIS-2. *Lancet*, 1, 397–402.

Italian Group for the Study of Streptokinase in Myocardial Infarction (GISSI) (1986). Effectiveness of intravenous thrombolytic treatment in acute myocardial infarction. *Lancet*, 22(8478), 397–402.

Joshi, PI, JJ Dalal, MS Ruttley, DJ Sheridan and AH Henderson (1981). Nifedipine and left ventricular function in beta-blocked patients. *British Heart Journal*, 45(4), 457–459.

Julian, DG (2001). The evolution of the coronary care unit. *Cardiovascular Research*, 51(4), 621–624.

Kang, PM, AJ Landou, RT Eberhardt and WH Frishman (1994). Angiotensin II receptor antagonists: A new approach to blockade of the renin-angiotensin system. *American Heart Journal*, 127, 1388–1401.

Kay, N, A Epstein and S Dailey (1992). Selective radiofrequency ablation of the slow pathway for the treatment of atrioventricular nodal re-entrant tachycardia. *Circulation*, 85, 1675–1688.

Keidel, WD (1950). New method of recording changes in volume of the human heart. *Zeitschrift fur Kreislaufforschung*, 39(9–10), 257–271.

Lands, AM, A Arnold, JA McAuliff, FP Luduena and TG Brown Jr (1967). Differentiation of receptor systems activated by sympathomimetic amines. *Nature*, 214, 597–598.

Mark, AL (1995). Sympathetic dysregulation in heart failure; mechanisms and therapy. *Clinical Cardiology*, 18(Suppl. I), I-3–I-8.

Mock, MB, I Ringqvist, LD Fisher, KB Davis, BR Chaitman, NT Kouchoukos, GC Kaiser, E Alderman, TJ Ryan, RO Russell, Jr, S Mullin, D Fray and T Killip 3rd (1982). Survival of medically treated patients in the coronary artery Surgery Study (CASS) Registry. *Circulation*, 66, 562–568.

Morice, MC, PW Serruys, JE Sausa, J Fajadet, E Ban Hayashi, M Perin, A Colombo, G Schuler, P Barragan, G Guagliumi, F Molnar and R Falotico (2002). RAVEL Study Group. Randomized Study with the Sirolimus-Coated Bx Velocity Balloon-Expandable Stent in the Treatment of Patients with de Novo Native Coronary Artery

Lesions. A randomized comparison of a sirolemus-eluting stent with a standard stent for coronary revascularization. *The New England Journal of Medicine*, 346, 1773–1780.

Murray, CJL and AD Lopez (1997). Regional patterns of disability-free life expectancy: global burden of disease study. *Lancet*, 349, 1347–1352.

Rentrop, KP, H Blanke, KR Karsh and H Kreuzer (1979). Initial experience with transluminal recanalisation of the recently occluded infarct related coronary artery in acute myocardial infarction: comparison with conventionally treated patients. *Clinical Cardiology*, 2, 92–105.

Ringer, S (1887). Concerning the action of calcium, potassium, and sodium salts upon the Eel's heart and upon the skeletal muscles of the frog. *Journal of Physiology*, 8, 15–19.

Rinkenberger, RL, EN Prystowsky, JJ Heger, PJ Troup, WM Jackman and D Zipes (1980). Effects of intravenous and chronic oral verapamil administration in patients with supraventricular tachyarrhythmias. *Circulation*, 62, 996–1010.

Rolf Smith, S, MJ Kendall, DJ Worthington and R Holder (1983). Can the biochemical responses to a beta 2-adrenoceptor stimulant be used to assess selectivity of beta-adrenoceptor blockers? *British Journal of Clinical Pharmacology*, 16, 557–560.

Ryan, TJ (2002). The coronary angiogram and its seminal contributions to cardiovascular medicine over five decades. *Circulation*, 106, 752–756.

Scandinavian Simvastatin Survival Study Group (1994). Randomised trial of cholesterol lowering in 4444 patients with coronary heart disease: the Scandinavian Simvastatin Survival Study (4S). *Lancet*, 344, 1383–1389.

Serruys, PW, P de Jaegere, F Kiemeneeij, C Macaya, W Rutsch, G Heyndrickx, H Emanuelsson, J Marco, V Legrand and P Materne (1994). A comparison of balloon-expandable-stent implantation with balloon angioplasty in patients with coronary artery disease. Benestent Study Group. *The New England Journal of Medicine*, 331, 485–495.

Sever, PS, B Dahlof, NR Poulter, H Wedel, G Beevers, M Caulfield, R Collins, SE Kjeldsen, A Kristinsson, GT McInnes, J Mehlsen, M Nieminen, E O'Brien and J Ostergren, for the ASCOT investigators (2003). Prevention of coronary and stroke events with atorvastatin in hypertensive patients who have average or lower that average cholesterol concentrations, in the Anglo-Scandinavian Cardiac Outcomes trial — Lipid lowering arm (ASCOT-LLA); a multicentre randomized controlled trial. *Lancet*, 361, 1149–1158.

Strauss, WE, T Fortin, P Hartigan, ED Folland and AF Parisi (1995). A comparison of quality of life scores in patients with angina pectoris after angioplasty compared with after medical therapy. Outcomes of a randomized clinical trial. Veterans Affairs Study of Angioplasty Compared to Medical Therapy Investigators. *Circulation*, 92(7), 1710–1719.

Svedmyr, N (1985). Fentorol: a beta 2-adrenergic agonist for use in asthma; pharmacology, pharmakinetics, clinical efficacy and adverse effects. *Pharmacotherapy*, 5, 109–126.

Tillet, WS and RL Garner (1933). The fibrinolytic activity of streptococci. *Journal of Experimental Medicine*, 58, 485.

Tillet, WS and S Sherry (1949). The effect in patients of streptococcal fibrinolysin (strep-tokinase) and streptococcal desoxyribonucease on fibrinous, purulent and sanguinous pleural exudations. *The Journal of Clinical Investigation*, 28, 173.

Tobis, JM, JA Mallery, J Gessert, J Griffith, D Mahon, M Bessen, M Moriuchi, L McLeay, M McRae and WL Henry (1989). Intravascular ultrasound cross-sectional arterial imaging before and after balloon angioplasty in vitro. *Circulation*, 80, 873–882.

Waller, AD (1887). A demonstration on man of electromotive changes accompanying the heart's beat. *The Journal Physiology (London)*, 8, 229–234.

Yusef, S, P Sleight, J Pogue, J Bosch, R Davies and G Dagenais (2000). Effects of an angiotensin converting enzyme inhibitor, ramapril on cardiovascular events in high risk patients. The Heart Outcomes Prevention Evaluation Study Investigation. *The New England Journal of Medicine*, 342, 145–153.

DEVELOPMENT AND INNOVATION IN CANCER MEDICINE

KAROL SIKORA

Buckingham School of Medicine, The University of Buckingham
Hunter Street, Buckingham MK18 1EG, UK
karolsikora@hotmail.com

Great strides have been made in the field of cancer medicine towards understanding the fundamental biology of cancers. Impressive treatments have emerged, resulting in markedly prolonged survival for many patients. These advances mean that, within the next 20 years, cancer could become a chronic disease rather than a death warrant. But that promise depends on sustained investment in innovation, and on society's willingness to pay for that innovation.

Realising this promise might be a problem for Europe where investment in medical science remains low compared to the United States which is driving global innovation in cancer technology (providing 55% of global funding for cancer although it only has 5% of the global cancer population) and where innovation is rewarded.

If Europe is to continue to play a leading role in cancer medicine, it needs greater investment in R&D with an environment that supports and rewards innovation.

Keywords: Cancer medicine; future scenarios; professional reconfiguration; new therapies.

Introduction

The age of the world's population is rising dramatically. This means that the total burden of cancer also increases, as many patients live longer with considerable co-morbidity. At the same time, new technology in many areas of medicine is improving the quality and length of life. Innovations in the following six areas are likely to have the most impact on cancer:

1. Molecularly targeted drugs with associated sophisticated diagnostic systems to personalise care.
2. Biosensors to detect, monitor and correct abnormal physiology, and to provide surrogate measurements of cancer risk.

45

3. Our ability to modify the human genome through systemically administered novel targeted vectors.
4. The continued miniaturisation of surgical intervention through robotics, nanotechnology and precise imaging.
5. Computer-driven interactive devices to help with everyday living.
6. The use of virtual reality systems which together with novel mood control drugs will create the illusion of wellness.

Over the last 20 years, a large amount of detailed data has been amassed concerning the basic biological processes that are disturbed by the onset of cancer. Today, we know the key elements involved in growth factor binding, signal transduction, gene transcription control, cell cycle checkpoints, apoptosis and angiogenesis (Sikora, 2002). These have become fertile areas to hunt for rationally based anti-cancer drugs. This approach has already led to a record number of novel compounds currently in trials. Targeted drugs such as rituximab, Herceptin®, imatinib, gefitinib, Avastin® and Erbitux® are all now in routine clinical use. Over the next decade, there will be a marked shift in the types of agents that are used for the systemic treatment of cancer.

Since we know the precise targets of these new agents, there will be a revolution in the way that we prescribe cancer therapy. Instead of defining drugs for use empirically and relatively ineffectively for different types of cancer, we will identify a series of molecular lesions in tumour biopsies. Future patients will receive drugs that directly target these lesions. The human genome project provides vast comparative information about normal and malignant cells. New therapies will be more selective and less toxic, and will be given for prolonged periods of time, even in some cases for the rest of a patient's life. This will lead to a radical overhaul in how we provide cancer care (The Stationery Office, 2003).

Investment in more sophisticated diagnostics is now required. Holistic systems such as genomics, proteomics, metabolomics and methylomics provide fascinating clues that will help us find the needle in the haystack of disturbed growth. By developing simple, reproducible and cheap assays for specific biomarkers, a battery of companion diagnostics will emerge (Nicolette and Miller, 2003). In the next decade, it is likely that these diagnostics will be firmly rooted in tissue pathology, making today's histopathologist essential to the forward movement of this exciting field. Ultimately, the fusion of tissue analysis with imaging technologies might make it possible to do virtual biopsies on any part of the body, normal and diseased alike (Adam *et al.*, 2002).

Individual risk assessment for cancer will lead to tailored prevention messages and a specific screening programme designed to pick up early cancer, with far-reaching consequences for public health. Cancer-preventive drugs will be developed to reduce the risk of further genetic deterioration. The use of gene arrays to monitor serum for fragments of DNA containing defined mutations could ultimately develop into an implanted gene chip. When a significant mutation is detected, the chip would signal the holder's home computer and set off a series of investigations based on the most likely type and site of the primary tumour.

As a result of improved survival, there will be an increase in the total prevalence of cancer, as well as change of cancer types to those with longer survival, such as prostate cancer. New challenges will be created in terms of assessing the risk of recurrence, designing care pathways, use of IT and improvement of service access. As experience grows with risk factors over the long term, there will be new opportunities for further targeting and development of existing therapies. Carefully monitoring a patient's experiences might help to improve results. Cancer might soon become a long-term management issue for many patients, who would be able to enjoy a high quality of life despite having a chronic illness (Tritter and Calnan, 2002).

Cancer care funding will become a significant problem (Bosanquet and Sikora, 2006). We are already seeing inequity in access to taxanes for breast and ovarian cancer, and to gemcitabine for lung and pancreatic cancer. These drugs are merely palliative. They only add a few months to life. The emerging compounds are likely to be far more successful, and their long-term administration to be considerably more expensive. Increasing consumerism in medicine will lead to more informed and assertive patients who seek out novel therapies and bypass traditional referral pathways by using global information networks. It is likely that integrated molecular solutions for cancer will develop, but unless issues related to access are addressed, this development will lead to far greater inequity than we currently have. Cost effectiveness analyses will scrutinise novel diagnostic technology and therapies.

The past

The first recorded reference to cancer was in the Edwin Smith Papyrus of 3,000 BC, in which eight women are described as having breast cancer. The writings of Hippocrates in 400 BC contain several descriptions of cancer occurring in various sites. But our understanding of the disease really began in the 19th century, with the advent of cellular pathology.

Successful treatment through radical surgery became possible in the later part of the 19th century due to advances in anaesthetics and antiseptics. Radical surgery involved the removal of the tumour-containing organ along with its draining lymph nodes in one block. Halstead in Johns Hopkins was the main protagonist of the radical mastectomy, Wertheim the hysterectomy, Trotter the pharyngectomy and Miles the abdomino-perineal resection of the rectum. These diverse surgical procedures all followed the same principles. When the 20th century ended, organs could

Table 1. Cancer timeline.

Date	Event
3000 BC	First recorded description
400 BC	Hippocrates describes six cancer types
1880	Successful radical mastectomy
1896	Oophorectomy for breast cancer
1898	Discovery of radium
1899	Discovery of X rays
1946	First publication on successful chemotherapy for cancer
1953	Double helical structure of DNA elucidated
1955	Successful use of combination chemotherapy
1999	First molecularly targeted therapy approved for use
2000	Human genome mapped

be conserved by minimising the destruction caused by surgery. Radiotherapy was often used instead, and for some sites, effective adjuvant therapy with drugs was used.

Radiotherapy has come a long way since the first patient with a nasal tumour was treated in 1899 (only 1 year after the discovery of radium by Marie Curie). Although radiobiology developed as a research discipline, its contributions to clinical practice have been minimal. The rationale behind modern fractionated radiotherapy comes as much out of empirical trial and error as it comes out of experimental results. For certain areas of the body, radiotherapy is remarkably successful. Increased sophistication in equipment coupled with dramatic strides in imaging, have led to great precision in planning and execution of treatment. Critical normal tissues are thus spared, and the dose to the tumour is increased (Table 1).

The sinking of the US battleship John B Harvey in Bari harbour by the Germans in 1942 led to the development of effective chemotherapy. The warship was carrying canisters of mustard gas for use in chemical warfare. When survivors developed leucopenia, Goodman and others in the US experimented with halogenated alkylamines in patients with high white cell counts: lymphomas, leukaemias and Hodgkin's disease. Since the first publication in 1946, the field has blossomed to the point where there are now over 200 drugs available in our global pharmacopoeia. But as in radiotherapy, our clinical practice is mainly based on empiricism (Symonds, 2001). Most of the currently used drugs are derived serendipitously from plants or fungi (taxol, vincristine, doxorubicin), rather than from rational drug design. Although these drugs were successfully used in combination for lymphoma, leukaemia, choriocarcinoma, testicular cancer and several childhood cancers, the results in metastatic common solid tumours have been disappointing, as they have been shown to have

high CR	high CR	low CR
high cure	*low cure*	*low cure*
5%	*40%*	*55%*
HD	AML	NSCLC
ALL	breast	colon
testis	ovary	stomach
chorio	SCLC	prostate
childhood	sarcoma	pancreas
BL	myeloma	glioma

Fig. 1. Chemotherapy for advanced cancer. There are three groups of cancer. The first group represents cancer which is frequently cured by drugs that have a high complete response (CR). In the second group, although there is a high CR, most patients relapse with resistant disease. In the third group, CR is rare; 5% of cancer patients are in the first group, 40% in the second and 55% in the third.

little more than palliative benefit (Fig. 1). The advent of molecularly targeted drugs promises to dramatically change all of this.

The future

Within the next 20 years, cancer will be considered a chronic disease, just like conditions such as diabetes, heart disease and asthma. These conditions impact the way people live but do not inevitably lead to death. The model of prostate cancer will become more usual: men die with it, not from it. Progress will be made in cancer prevention, and also in enhancement of our understanding of the causes of cancer. Our concepts then will be different than they are today. New types of cancer detection, diagnosis and treatment will be crucial to understand the future.

When cancer develops, it will be controllable due to refinements of current technologies and techniques (imaging, radiotherapy and surgery), and availability of targeted drugs. A cure will still be sought, but will not be the only satisfactory outcome. Patients will still be closely monitored after treatment but the fear that is prevalent even in the beginning of the 21st century, that cancer inevitably kills, will be replaced by an acceptance that many forms of cancer are a consequence of old age.

Making predictions about the future is fraught with difficulties. In the 1980s, who could have imagined the impact that mobile phones, the internet and low-cost airlines would have on global communication? Medicine will progress by similar unexpected, incremental changes in innovation.

Therefore, it is difficult to analyse the economic impact of developments in cancer care. The greatest benefit will simply be the assurance that the best possible care is offered to the most patients, irrespective of their socio-economic circumstances and of any scientific developments. This is an unrealistic prediction. Technologies are developing fast, particularly in the imaging and exploitation of the human genome. Well-informed patients who have adequate funds will always have rapid access to the newest and the best products, no matter where in the world they may be found. More patients will benefit from better diagnosis and newer treatments, with greater emphasis on quality of life (Laing, 2002). Innovation will bring even more inequality to health if the parties involved do not work together to ensure that they address the challenges of access. Today, outcomes of the same quality of care vary between socio-economic groups, and they will continue to do so in the future.

European clinicians will continue being dependent on technologies that are designed primarily for the world's biggest health market — the United States, which currently consumes nearly 55% of cancer medication but contains less than 5% of the cancer population. European legislation covering clinical trials could bring research in the UK to a grinding halt. Ethicists who zealously interpret privacy legislation could impose restrictions on the use of tissue. Targeted niche drugs will be less appealing to industry because the costs of bringing each new generation of drugs to market will not be matched by the returns from current blockbusters. The delivery of innovation will be underpinned by patient expectation. Well-informed patients will be equal partners in choosing the health care they receive. Much of it will take place close to their homes, and use mechanisms that are devised by innovative service providers (World Cancer Report, 2003).

This has huge implications for the training of health professionals and the demarcations between specialties. Emerging technologies will drive change. Intra-professional boundaries will be blurred. Doctors from what were traditionally quite distinct specialties might find themselves doing the same job. Clinical responsibilities will be taken up by health professionals who are not medically qualified. All professionals are likely to find challenges to their territory hard to accept. Table 2 shows the challenges that must be addressed in order to deliver the most health benefits.

Table 2. The challenges of cancer care.

Increasing the focus on prevention
Improving screening and diagnosis, and their impact on treatment
New targeted treatments — how effective and affordable will they be?
How will patients' and caregivers' expectations translate into delivery?
Reconfiguring health services to deliver optimal care
The impact of reconfiguration on professional territories
Will society accept the financial burden of these opportunities?

Prevention and Screening

In the early years of the 21st century, 10 million people each year develop cancer worldwide (Blackledge, 2003). The causes of these cancers are known in roughly 75% of cases: 3 million are tobacco-related; 3 million are a result of diet; and 1.5 million are caused by infection. In the UK, 120,000 people die from cancer each year, even though many of these cancers are preventable — with one-third related to smoking. Still, only 2% of the total funding on cancer care and research is spent on cancer prevention. Anti-smoking initiatives are considered successful — even though it has been 50 years since the association between smoking and cancer was first identified. In the 1960s, 80% of the population smoked. In 2005, that average was less than 30%. These figures mask real health inequality. The percentage of smokers among higher socio-economic classes is low (in single figures), while the percentage among lower socio-economic classes is around 50% in some parts of the country. Although the risks are known, it remains true that if friends and family smoke and there is no social pressure to stop, there is no incentive. A ban on smoking in public places leads to a further drop of around 4%. Tax increases have been a powerful incentive to stop smoking, but the price of a packet of cigarettes became so high that smokers turned to the black market: as many as one in five cigarettes smoked is smuggled into the country. Lung cancer is now a rare disease in higher socio-economic groups; it is primarily a disease of poverty.

Lessons taken from anti-smoking initiatives will be instructive for future prevention. Although the association of poor diet, obesity and lack of exercise with cancer has not yet been confirmed, there is sufficient circumstantial evidence to suggest that associations will be found. A ban will be put on television advertising for crisps, sweets and soft drinks, a health tax will be put on these products, and there will be a ban on sponsorship of public events by manufacturers of these products. By 2010, obesity among the middle classes will be socially unacceptable, but among the economically disadvantaged it will not change. A major challenge that lies ahead is the creation of meaningful, imaginative incentives for people to adopt healthy lifestyles.

The future prevention picture will be coloured by post-genomic research. In 2005, it is accepted among the medical community that about 100 genes are associated with the development of a wide range of cancers. The detection of polymorphisms in low penetrance cancer-related genes (or a combination of changed genes) will identify people who run an increased risk. Within the next 20 years, most people will be genetically mapped. The information gained from a simple blood test will easily be stored on a smart-card. Legislation will be required to prevent this information from being used to determine an individual's future health status for mortgage, insurance and employment purposes. However, the mapping process will

Table 3. Balancing cancer risk.

Great health inequity exists among smoking-related diseases
Novel prevention strategies are likely to lead to similar inequity
The creation of meaningful incentives to reduce risks will be essential
Individually tailored messages will have a greater power to change lifestyles
Biomarkers of risk will enhance the validation of cancer preventive drugs
Novel providers of risk assessment and correction will emerge

reveal that every person screened has a predisposition to certain diseases. People will have to learn to live with risk.

Today the average age of a patient diagnosed with cancer, is 68. Improvements in screening, detection and diagnosis will reduce that number. A predisposition for cancers that manifest in a patient's 70s or 80s will be found out in a patient's young adult life, and corrected successfully before the patient reaches his or her 40s. Age increase will remain the strongest risk predictor. Most of what has been described is already happening in some form, but the computing power that will be used in the future to calculate risk and predictions, will be unimaginable in scale. Screening programmes will be developed on a national basis as long as they are simple, robust and cheap. Patients will expect the screening venues to be convenient places such as shopping malls. They will also expect screenings not to be painful or overly time-consuming. Health professionals will insist that any programme is accurate and does not give misleading results. Governments will insist that a programme's costs lead to more effective use of other resources. Novel providers of risk assessment services will likely emerge (Table 3).

Detecting Cancer

Cancers are fundamentally somatic genetic diseases which result from several types of causes: physical, viral, radiation and chemical damage, chronic inflammatory change, immuno-surveillance, and failure of apoptosis. In the future, cancer will not be looked at as a single entity, it will be considered a cellular process that changes over time. Many diseases that are today labelled as cancer will be renamed because their development will not reflect the new paradigm. Patients will not accept cancer as a single disease. Increasingly, they will come to understand it as a cellular process. Many more elderly people will have increased risk or some type of precancer. This has huge implications for cancer services. Today, most diagnoses of cancer depend on human interpretation of changes in cell structures seen down a microscope. Microscopes will soon be superseded by a new generation of scanners to detect molecular changes. These scanners will build up a picture of change over time, imaging cellular activity rather than just a single snapshot. We will be able to probe the molecular events that are markers for early malignant change. This dynamic imaging will lead to more sensitive screening and treatments. Imaging agents will accumulate in cells exhibiting tell-tale signs of pre-cancer activity, and will be used to introduce treatment agents directly (Brumley, 2002).

Imaging and diagnosis will be minimally invasive and enable the selection of the best and most effective targeted treatment (Table 4). Better imaging will be able to pick up pre-disease phases and deal with them before they are currently detectable. These techniques will be crucial in successful follow-up. A patient with a predisposition to a certain cancer process will be monitored regularly, and treatment will be offered when necessary. Not all cancers will be diagnosed in these early stages. Inevitably, some patients will fall through the screening net. Nevertheless, there will be more opportunities than there are at present to offer less invasive treatment. Surgery and radiotherapy will continue but in greatly modified form as a result of developments in imaging. Most significantly, surgery will become a part of integrated care. Removal of tumours, or even of whole organs, will still occasionally be necessary. The difference is that the surgeon will be supported by 3-D imaging, by radio-labelling techniques to guide incisions, and by robotic instruments. Although many of the new treatments made possible by improved imaging will be biologically driven, radiotherapy will still play a role. It will always be the most potent DNA damaging agent for treating cancer with the most geographical accuracy. Radiotherapy targeting will be greatly enhanced, and treatment will be more precise.

In addition to the reconfiguration and merging of the clinicians' skills, the delivery of care will also change. Minimally invasive treatments will reduce the need for long hospital stays. It will not only be possible for patients to receive care close to their homes, as this report will show later on, it will be expected. The prospect of highly sophisticated scanning equipment and mobile surgical units that can be transported to where they are needed, is not unrealistic. Technicians, surgical assistants and nurses would provide the hands-on care, and technical support will be provided by a new breed of clinician — a disease-specific imaging specialist who works from a remote site. Cost control will be an essential component of the diagnostic phase.

Table 4. Innovation in diagnostics.

Radiology and pathology will merge into cancer imaging
Dynamic imaging will create a changing image of biochemical abnormalities
Cancer changes will be detected prior to disease spread from the primary site
Greater precision in surgery and radiotherapy will be used for pre-cancer
Molecular signatures will determine treatment choice
Cost control will be essential for healthcare payers to avoid inefficient diagnostics

Healthcare payers will create sophisticated systems for evaluating the economic benefits of innovative imaging and tissue analysis technology.

New Treatment Approaches

Future cancer care will be driven by the least invasive therapy that is consistent with long-term survival. Eradication, although still desirable, will no longer be the primary aim of treatment. Cancers will be identified earlier and the disease process will be regulated in a similar way to chronic diseases such as diabetes. Surgery and radiotherapy will still play a role, how great a role will depend on the type of cancer a patient has, the stage at which the disease is identified, and how well the drugs that are currently in development perform in the future.

Cancer treatment will be shaped by a new generation of drugs. What that generation will look like depends critically on the relative success of agents that are currently in development, and on society's willingness to pay for innovation. Over the next three to five years we will begin to understand better the benefits that compounds such as kinase inhibitors are likely to provide. It is estimated that around 500 drugs are currently being tested in clinical trials. Around 300 of these drugs inhibit specific molecular targets (Melzer, 2003), but that number is set to rise dramatically. By 2007, 2,000 compounds will be available to enter clinical trials, and by 2010, that number will increase to 5,000. Many of these drug candidates will be directed at the same molecular targets, so industry is racing to screen those that are most likely to make it through the development process. By 2008, tremendous pressures will come from the loss of patent protection for the majority of high-cost chemotherapy drugs. Unless new premium-priced innovative drugs are made available, cancer drug provision will come from global generic manufacturers who are currently gearing up for this change.

What will these drug candidates look like? The main focus of current research is on small molecules which are designed to target the specific gene products that control the biological processes associated with cancer. These include signal transduction, angiogenesis, cell cycle control, apoptosis, inflammation, invasion and differentiation. Treatment strategies that involve monoclonal antibodies, cancer vaccines, and gene therapy are also being explored. Although we do not know exactly what these targeted agents will look like, there is growing confidence that they will work. What is more uncertain is their overall efficacy at prolonging survival. Many might be no more than expensive palliatives. In the future, advances will be driven by a better biological understanding of the disease process (Fig. 2).

We are already seeing the emergence of drugs targeted at the molecular level: Herceptin®, directed at the HER2 protein, Glivec®, which targets the Bcr-Abl tyrosine kinase, and Iressa® and Tarceva®, directed at EGFR tyrosine kinase. These

base case launch years in the US

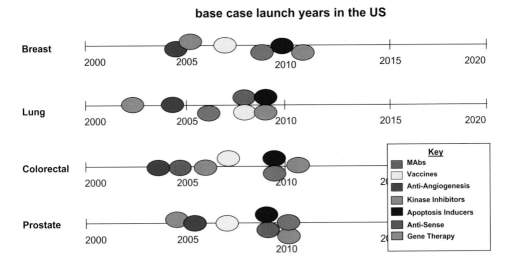

Fig. 2. Predicted new drug application (NDA) dates for molecular therapies in the USA. The years 2005–2010 will see an explosion of novel therapies coming into clinical use outside of the research setting (MAb = molecular antibodies).

therapies will be used across a range of cancers. In the future, it will be important to know whether a person's cancer has particular biological or genetic characteristics. Traditional categories will continue to be broken down, and genetic profiling will enable treatments to be targeted towards the right patients. Patients will understand that their treatment options depend on their genetic profile. The risks and benefits of treatment will be much more predictable than they are today (Table 5).

Therapies will emerge through our knowledge of the human genome and the use of sophisticated bioinformatics. Targeted imaging agents will be used to deliver therapy at the time of screening or diagnosis. The way that cancer patients are monitored will also change, as technology allows for closer tracking of the disease process. Treatment strategies will reflect this, and drug resistance will become

Table 5. Drivers of molecular therapeutics.

HGP and bioinformatics
Expression vectors for target production
In silico drug design
Robotic high throughput screening
Combinatorial chemistry
Platform approach to drug discovery
Huge increase in number of molecular targets

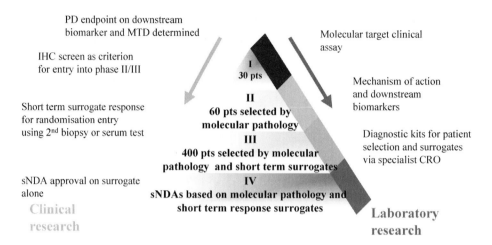

Fig. 3.   The future of cancer drug development. For the first time, drugs will be administered to patients accompanied by effective biomarkers. These in turn will be used to identify surrogate markers of response, and therefore selecting the patients early in pivotal studies who should either continue or stop a specific trial. In addition to this, continued laboratory research will be used to create diagnostic kits which will identify signatures of response. (Pts = Patients; PD = Pharmacodynamic; MTD = Maximum Tolerated Dose; IHC = Immunohistochemistry; sNDA = Supplemental New Drug Application; CRO = Contract Research Organisation).

much more predictable. Biomarkers will allow those who treat people for cancer to measure a drug's effect on its target. If it is not working, an alternative treatment strategy will be sought. Tumour regression will become less important as clinicians look for molecular patterns and responses of disease (Fig. 3).

There will be more of a focus on cancer-preventing therapies. A tangible risk indicator and risk reducing therapy, along the lines of cholesterol and statins, would allow people to monitor their risk and intervene when necessary. Delivering treatment early in the disease process will also be made possible as subtle changes in cellular activity become detectable, leading to less aggressive treatment. The role that the industry plays in the development of new therapies will continue to change. Smaller, more specialised companies that are affiliated with universities will increasingly deliver drug candidates and innovative diagnostics to 'Big Pharma' for development and marketing (Fig. 4).

People will become used to living with risk, and they will have more knowledge about their propensity for disease. Programmes will enable people to determine their own predisposition to cancer. This, in turn, will encourage health-changing behaviour and lead people to seek out information about the treatment options that are available to them. As medicine becomes more personalised, patients will become more involved in decision-making. Indeed, doctors may find themselves directed

Diagnostic	Value
Predisposition screen	Identify patients for chemo-prevention
Screen for presence of cancer	Increase in patients - earlier disease
Pharmacodynamic biomarker	Establish pharmacological dose
Surrogate marker of clinical efficacy	Early indication of proof of concept
Predictive reclassification of disease	Target therapy to those likely to respond
Patient-specific toxicity prediction	Avoid adverse events, adjust dose

Fig. 4. Cancer diagnostics in drug development. There are six areas where diagnostics could help to personalise cancer medicine.

Table 6. The uncertainty of novel drugs for cancer.

Will the new generation of small molecule kinase inhibitors really make a difference, or just be expensive palliation?

How will big pharma cope with most high value cytotoxics becoming generic by 2008?

Can expensive late stage attrition really be avoided in cancer drug development?

How will sophisticated molecular diagnostic services be provided?

Will effective surrogates for cancer preventive agents emerge?

Will patient choice involve cost considerations in guiding therapy?

by well-informed patients. All of this coupled with an environment where patients are able to demonstrate choice, will help drive innovation towards those who stand to benefit from it. However, inequity based on education, wealth and access will still continue (Table 6).

Barriers to Innovation

Innovation in cancer treatment is inevitable (Dixon *et al.* 2003). The nature and intensity of treatment will be critically influenced by the way innovation is rewarded. However, there are certain prerequisites for the introduction of new therapies. First, innovation must be translated into usable therapies that must be deliverable to the right biological target, and to the right patient in a way that is acceptable to the patient, the healthcare professional and society. Innovation must also be marketed successfully to professionals, patients and those who pay the cost, so that they all understand the potential benefits. Those making the investments in research will create a market for innovation, even if the benefits achieved are minimal. The

Drug (brand name)	Generic name	Manufacturer	Yearly cost of treating a patient
Herceptin	traztuzumab	Roche	£60K
Mabthera	rituximab	Roche	£40K
Glivec	imatinib	Novartis	£50K
Erbitux	cetuximab	BMS	£60K
Avastin	bevacizumab	Genentech	£70K
Tarceva	erlotinib	Roche	£65K
Iressa	gefitinib	AZ	£40K

Fig. 5. Marketed targeted therapies showing their high cost.

explosion of new therapies in cancer care will continue, and pricing of these drugs will remain high. The cost of cancer drugs in 2005 is estimated to be $24bn globally. Of that amount, $15bn is spent in the United States. If effective drugs emerge from the research and development pipeline, the cancer drug market could reach $300bn globally by 2025, with this cost spreading more widely around the world (Fig. 5).

Paralleling the explosion in therapies and the increase in costs, a number of confounding factors will make markets smaller (Locock *et al.*, 2003). Technology will reveal which patients will not respond to therapy. Hence, blockbuster drugs will be made obsolete. Doctors will know the precise stage in the disease process where treatment is necessary. As cancer becomes a chronic disease, people will have more co-morbidities, bringing associated drug-drug interactions and increasing care requirements.

How do we balance this equation? The pharmaceutical companies will not necessarily want to do the studies to fragment their market. Research that leads to rational rationing will need to be driven by health care payers. There is a risk that pharmaceutical companies could stop developing cancer drugs and begin to focus instead on therapeutic areas that have less individual variation and therefore more scope for profit. Furthermore, development costs are rising. Ten years ago, the average cost of developing a new cancer drug was around $400m. Today it is around $1bn. At this rate of growth, the cost of developing a new drug could soon reach $2bn, an amount that would be unsustainable in a shrinking market. With all this in mind, the process of drug development must be made faster.

Instead of simplifying research, changes in legislation concerning privacy and prior consent make research more difficult. The EU Clinical Trials Directive will make it impossible to have quick hypothesis-testing trials. Other challenges exist as well, such as obtaining consent for new uses of existing human tissue — following political anxiety when consent for removing and storing tissues had not been obtained in the early years of the 21st century. However, surveys have shown

Table 7. Barriers to innovation.

The drug industry will continue to compete for investment in a competitive, capitalist environment

Blockbuster drugs drive profit — niche products are unattractive in today's market

Personalised therapies are difficult for today's industry machine

Surrogate endpoints will be essential to register new drugs

Novel providers will emerge providing both diagnostic and therapy services

Payers will seek robust justification for the use of high cost agents

---

that patients who gave their consent for tissue to be used for a certain purpose did not mind if it was used for another. Patients do not like to be reminded of their cancer years after they have been cured. In order to overcome these constraints, regulators who approve therapies will have to accept surrogate markers, rather than clinical outcomes. Outcome studies might move to a post-registration surveillance of a drug's efficacy, similar to cholesterol lowering agents today.

The rise of personalised medicine will mean that the temptation to over-treat will disappear. Doctors and patients will know whether or not a particular treatment is justified because the evidence will be there to support their decisions. Therefore, treatment failure, along with its associated costs, will become less common (Table 7).

Patient's Experience

Two separate developments will determine a patient's cancer care experience in future. The increasing expectations of patients as consumers will cause health services to become more responsive to the individual, similar to the way other service industries already are. Targeted approaches to diagnosis and treatment will individualise care. People will have higher personal expectations, will be less deferential to professionals, and will be more willing to seek alternative care providers if they are dissatisfied. As a result, patients will be more involved in their care. They will take more responsibility for their health decisions, rather than adopt a paternalistic "doctor knows best" attitude. These changes will partly be fuelled by the internet and by competitive provider systems. By 2025, the majority of people in their 70s and 80s will be adept at using the internet to access information (Institute of Medicine, 2001).

As patients begin to have access to all this health information, they will need people who can interpret the huge amounts of information available, help them to assess risks and benefits, and determine what is relevant for them. These patient brokers will be compassionate, independent advocates who will act as patients' guides through the system. They will be aided by intelligent algorithms to ensure that patients understand their screenings and the implications of early diagnosis. They will spell out the meaning of genetic susceptibility, and they will guide patients through their treatment options. Patients and health professionals will trust in computer-aided decision making because of the evidence they will have that the programmes work.

The way the service will be designed around patients' needs and expectations will be determined by the available improved treatments and their individualisation. In early stages of the disease, care will be available close to where patients live. Even the most sophisticated diagnostic machinery and robotic surgeons will be mobile, so that intervention can be carried out by technicians and nurses, while the highly trained professionals at a distant base are in audio-visual contact. When cancer centres first developed in the mid-20th century, the diseases they treated were relatively rare, and survival was low. Although these centres concentrated expertise, being referred to one of them was distressing for some patients. Cancer will become a commonly accepted chronic condition. Even when inpatient care is required, patients will be able to choose from many "cancer hotels" around the world where they may receive care. But that option will not even be necessary for many patients. Patients may be treated in their own communities because most new drugs will be administered orally (West, 2003). However, this approach to cancer and other concomitant chronic conditions will place a huge burden on social services and families. Systems will be put in place to manage these diseases and conditions, psychologically as well as physically. Pain relief and control of other symptoms associated with cancer treatment will be much improved.

Seventy per cent of today's cancer budget is being spent on care in the last six months of patients' lives. Although many recognise that such treatment has more to do with managing fear than with managing cancer, medical professionals have relatively few treatment options available, and there is limited awareness as to which patients would benefit. There is also an industry-wide reluctance to do anything that would destroy a patient's hopes. This reluctance leads to confusion about the limits of conventional medicines and anxiety about facing the inevitable on the part of patients as well as their families and doctors. There is a widespread perception that patients who continue being offered anti-cancer treatment might have their health restored.

As better treatments emerge, consumers of services will be able to focus more on quality of life. Much of the fear that is now associated with cancer, will be mitigated. Demand will be high for treatments with fewer side effects or lower toxicity, even if these have only modest survival gains. The transition between active and palliative care is often sudden, but in future the change will be less apparent, because patients will have greater control over their own situation (Table 8).

Professional Reconfiguration

In the future, one of the greatest challenges to providing the best cancer care will be putting the right people into the right jobs. It will be essential to stop training

Table 8. The future cancer experience.

Patient brokers will guide patients who have cancer through the system
Choice will be real and will involve cost decisions
Patients will contribute to their care costs
Complementary therapies will be widely available and well-regulated
Themed death chosen by patients will be possible

people for jobs that will no longer exist. Policy makers have begun to grasp some of the workforce difficulties that lie ahead. They are making moves to ensure that healthcare professionals have responsibilities commensurate with their level of education and professional skills. Nurses and pharmacists are being encouraged to take over some of the responsibilities that have traditionally been held by doctors, such as prescribing. At the same time, the roles that have always been held by nurses and pharmacists are being given to technicians and other support staff.

Having the appropriate mix of skills will become critical. The barriers that have existed between healthcare professions will have to be broken down, so as to deliver new approaches to the care of patients with cancer and many other diseases. Intra-professional barriers will disappear. The work of pathologists and radiologists will be united, as their traditional skills are augmented by the new generation of diagnostic and treatment devices. Oncologists will find that many forms of chemotherapy will be delivered with the aid of new technology. And surgeons will use robots to operate. Fewer highly trained specialists will be required, since much of their responsibilities will be delegated to specialist technicians and nurses working to protocols. Furthermore, since the technology will be mobile and skills may be used remotely, highly trained individuals will have the capability to work at a number of sites on the same day. A number of factors will determine the balance between different skills. Some of these factors are the size of the medical workforce, the capacity of the system to provide care, and the availability of trained support staff (Table 9).

Table 9. Manpower considerations required to meet future needs.

The right person for the right job — key challenges
Planning the amount of manpower need for new technology
Doctors and other healthcare specialists
Prescribing of cancer drugs by nurses, pharmacists and others
Training the caregivers of elderly people with co-morbidities
Making patients equal partners in decision-making

Conclusion

In the future, cancer will become incidental to day to day living; although not erad-icated it will cause less anxiety for patients who will also be much better informed.

How true this picture will be will depend on whether the technological inno-vations will emerge. Will people, for example, really live in smart houses where their televisions play a critical role in monitoring their health and well being? For this to be a reality health care professionals will need to work in multidisciplinary teams in collaboration with caregivers and voluntary support groups to provide for an increasing older population in the context of a diminishing number of working age who pay taxes. Old people, having been relatively poor all their lives, may suffer from cancer and a wide range of co-morbidities that will limit their quality of life. Looking after everyone, rich and poor, will place great strains on healthcare funding and its provision.

As with all health issues the question of access will be determined by cost and political will. In 2005 about 70% of cancer care was incurred in the last six months of patients' lives and costs are set to rise about fourfold by 2025 as patients live longer and new therapies emerge. Recent surveys appear to support this level of spending, but is it likely to be affordable?

Expenditure at such levels will inevitably create tensions between appropriate levels of taxation and provision of health care. To some extent this will be mitigated by better targeting of expensive therapies, less use of hospitals beds in favour of home based care. However as patients live longer, life time costs will increase so that the prospect of rationing will remain.

One dilemma for the future will be the political power of old people. As more people live longer, this increasing gerontocracy will wield considerable influence and will have higher expectations than the level of care now offered to many old people. Will a tax-based health system, in the context of a decreasing number of people working and paying taxes, be able to fund their expectations or will a system of co-payments and deductibles become inevitable.

Figure 6 shows the four components of cancer's future — innovation, delivery, finances and society. Whatever system is put in place there is the prospect of a major socio-economic division in cancer care. A small percentage of the elderly population will have made personal provision for their retirement, in terms of health and welfare, but the vast majority will rely on state provision. Policy-makers need to start planning now as they are doing for the looming pensions crisis. Cancer patient and health advocacy groups need to be involved in the debate to ensure that difficult decisions are reached by consensus.

Societal changes will also create new challenges in the provision of care. A decline in hierarchical religious structures, a reduction in family integrity through

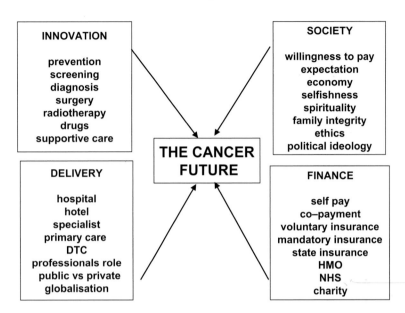

Fig. 6. The four building blocks of cancer's future — innovation, society, delivery and finances (DTC = Diagnostic and Treatment Centres; HMO = Health Maintenance Organisation; NHS = National Health Service).

increasing divorce, greater international mobility and the increased selfishness of a consumer driven culture will leave many isolated with little support at the onset of serious illness. There will be a global shortage of caregivers, who are the unskilled, low paid but essential component of any health delivery system and an invaluable human capital resource, for which there will be increasing competition.

New financial structures will emerge with novel consortia from the pharmaceutical, financial and healthcare sectors, which will enable people to buy into the level of care they wish to pay for. Cancer, cardiovascular disease and dementia will be controlled and join today's list of chronic diseases such as diabetes, asthma and hypertension. Hospitals will become attractive health hotels run by competing private sector providers. Global franchises will provide speciality therapies through these structures similar to the internationally branded shops in today's malls. Governments will have long ceased to deliver care. By the end of this decade, Britain's NHS, one of the last centralised systems to disappear, will convert to UK Health, a regulator and safety net insurer.

The ability of technology to improve cancer care is assured, but it will come at a price — namely, the direct costs of providing it and the costs of looking after the increasingly elderly population it will produce. New ethical and moral dilemmas will arise as we seek the holy grail of compressed morbidity. Living long and dying fast will become the mantra of 21st century medicine.

References

Adam, BL, Y Qu, JW Davis, MD Ward, MA Clements, LH Cazares, OJ Semmes, PF Schellhammer, Y Yasui, Z Feng and GL Wright Jr (2002). Serum protein fingerprinting coupled with a pattern-matching algorithm distinguishes prostate cancer from benign prostate hyperplasia and healthy men. *Cancer Research*, 62, 3609–3614.

Blackledge, G (2003). Cancer drugs: the next ten years. *European Journal of Cancer*, 39, 273.

Bosanquet, N and K Sikora (2006). *The Economics of Cancer Care*. Cambridge University Press: Cambridge.

Brumley, RD (2002). Future of end of life care: the managed care organisation perspective. *Journal of Palliative Medicine*, 5, 263–270.

The Stationery Office (2003). 2020 Vision: Our Future Healthcare Environments. Norwich: The Stationery Office.

Dixon, J, J Le Grand and P Smith (2003). *Shaping the New NHS: Can Market Forces be Used for Good?* London: King's Fund.

Institute of Medicine (2001). *Crossing the Quality Chasm: A New Health System for the 21st Century*. Washington, USA: National Academy Press.

Laing, A (2002). Meeting patient expectations: healthcare professionals and service re-engineering. *Health Services Management Research*, 15, 165-172.

Locock, L (2003). Redesigning health care: new wine from old bottles? *Journal of Health Services Research and Policy*, 8, 120–122.

Melzer, D (2003). *My Very Own Medicine: What Must I Know?* Cambridge.

Nicolette, CA and GA Miller (2003). The identification of clinically relevant markers and therapeutic targets. *Drug Discovery Today*, 8, 31–38.

Sikora K (2002). The impact of future technology on cancer care. *Clinical Medicine*, 2, 560–568.

Symonds, RP (2001). Radiotherapy. *BMJ*, 323, 1107–1110.

Department of Health (2000) *Shaping the Future NHS: Long Term Planning for Hospitals and Related Services*. London: Department of Health.

Tritter, JQ and N Calnan (2002). Cancer as a chronic illness? Reconsidering categorisation and exploring experience. *European Journal of Cancer*, 11, 161–165.

Wanless, D (2003). *Securing Good Health for the Whole Population*. London: Department of Health.

Watters JW and HL McLeod (2003). Cancer pharmacogenomics: current and future applications. *Biochimica et Biophysica Acta*, 1603, 99.

West, E (2003). *Nursing Workforce Issues*. London: Macmillan Cancer Relief.

World Cancer Report (2003). Lyons: IARC Press.

INNOVATION, PATENTS AND ECONOMIC GROWTH

RIFAT A. ATUN

Centre for Health Management, Tanaka Business School
Imperial College London, London, SW7 2AZ, UK
r.atun@imperial.ac.uk

IAN HARVEY

Intellectual Property Institute, London, UK

JOFF WILD

Intellectual Asset Management Magazine

Empirical evidence demonstrates the value of intellectual property (IP) in creating economic growth, enhancing productivity and profitability, and increasing enterprise value. Research and Development (R&D) intensive industries, such as the life sciences, where patents are critical to competition, need an enabling environment to institutionalise innovation and IP generation and reward investments in IP.

The US has approached IP strategically and created an IP infrastructure. Japan aims to develop into an "IP nation". China has an increasingly well-developed IP system. In contrast, the European Union (EU), which aims to become the world's leading knowledge-based economy, has a fragmented and expensive system of national patents. It lacks an environment which values investment in IP generation and management.

Until recently, the EU enjoyed global competitive advantage in the life sciences, but this advantage has been lost. To regain this competitive advantage the EU must invest substantially in R&D, IP generation and commercialisation of these outputs.

Keywords: Innovation; life sciences; patent systems; China; EU; USA; Japan.

Introduction

The Organisation for Economic Cooperation and Development (OECD) emphasises that long run economic growth depends on the creation and fostering of an environment that encourages innovation and application of new technologies. Innovative activity underpins economic productivity and growth. Countries that generate innovation, create new technologies, and encourage adoption of these new technologies grow faster than those that do not. Innovation is singled out as the likely factor that drives long-term productivity and economic growth (OECD, 2003, 2005a, c). Patents, one form of intellectual property (IP),[1] and the focus of this paper, are one of the most commonly used measures of innovation output.

For many industries, especially those that are Research and Development (R&D) intensive, IP is the key building block for product development and a critical determinant for investment decisions. An environment that safeguards IP encourages inventors and organisations to invest resources in R&D for technological innovation. In some industries patenting is identified as the most important means of protecting IP and is increasingly used as a strategic asset by companies to create sustainable competitive advantage — although, in others, secrecy is used to safeguard proprietary knowledge.

The importance of IP and patents is now widely recognised. For example the Lisbon Agenda has explicitly stressed the importance of innovation and IP for the European Union to meet its objective to become the most competitive knowledge-based economy in the world by 2010 (Commission of the European Communities, 2002). As with the EU, many countries are actively pursuing policies to develop appropriate IP infrastructures, as these are seen to be critical to business innovation, competition and economic growth. But as this paper will demonstrate, the extent to which effective policies are developed and the success of execution vary.

This paper draws on a review of published evidence and company case studies to explore the evidence linking innovation, IP, competitiveness and economic growth. The paper analyses policy initiatives in the US, Japan, China and the EU aimed at improving innovation, IP management and competitiveness. Through case studies, it illustrates successful strategies pursued by businesses to harness IP in order to enhance innovation and competitiveness. The paper concludes by discussing policy implications of these findings.

Patents and Intellectual Property

Broadly speaking, IP rights are legally enforceable rights relating to creations of the mind and include inventions, literary and artistic works, and symbols, names, images and designs used in commerce. A number of individual rights are covered by IP. Some of the most important are patents, trademarks, copyrights, designs and

---

[1] Others include trade marks, copyrights, designs, smells and trade secrets but are not discussed in this paper.

trade secrets (World Intellectual Property Institute, 2006). Patents and IP rights have been created as a society recognises the need to foster innovation and to reward the innovator.

A patent for an invention is granted by government to the inventor. When a patent is granted, that *right* becomes the property of the inventor, which — like any other form of property or business asset — can be bought, sold, rented or hired. A patent is a national right but one that must meet global criteria in order to be granted. The patent is not a monopoly, but gives the inventor the *right* — normally for 20 years from the date when the patent application was first filed — to stop others from making, using or selling the invention without the permission of the inventor.

The ability to protect rights to IP is a key criterion for investment decisions in many industrial sectors, such as the life sciences, where costs of R&D and commercialisation are very high and risk of failure substantial. But as the marginal cost of production is low, data protection is of critical importance.

Innovation, IP and Competitiveness: The Evidence and Arguments

Solow (1957) has demonstrated that technical progress — not just factor inputs of capital and labour — account for economic growth. Total factor productivity, also known as the growth residual and which includes innovation and technology application, represents output growth not accounted for by the increases in factor inputs. In the period 1970–1990, total factor productivity was the major driver of economic growth in the world: accounting for 41% of the total growth, as compared with 38% for capital and 21% for labour (OECD, 1998).

Many studies have explored the relationship between economic growth, competitiveness, innovation and IP. These studies have generally used R&D investment or the number of patents filed as proxies for innovation (Griliches, 1980; Mansfield, 1980; Scherer, 1982) and some of them are discussed below.

Country level studies

In their study for the UK Department for Trade and Industry, Porter and Ketels (Department of Trade and Industry and Economic and Social Research Council, 2003) argue that true competitiveness is measured by economic productivity — determined by capital intensity, labour force skills and total factor productivity — and productivity growth is influenced by trade, investment and innovative activity. They suggest that countries' economies, in terms of their characteristic competitive advantage and modes of competing, evolve through three consecutive stages. In the first "Factor-driven stage", characterised by a low wage environment, competitive advantage is based on the availability of labour and natural resources. In the second, "Investment-driven Stage", the competitive advantage is based on productive efficiency for standard products (which are exported) and services (which are outsourced by other countries). In the third "Innovation-driven Stage" in which the developed countries are situated, competitive advantage depends on the ability to produce and use innovative products and services. In this stage, the competitive landscape for companies differs from the two earlier stages in that innovation and IP are key drivers of country- and company-level competition and investment is critical to developing innovative capacity and using the latest technology (Department of Trade and Industry and Economic and Social Research Council, 2003).

Using compound annual growth rate of US-registered patents as an indicator of innovation output Porter and Ketels demonstrate that in the recent past UK innovation performance has been low in relation to key competitors. The authors highlight low UK investment levels in R&D and show an increasing gap in investment as compared to key competitors. They conclude the current levels of innovation in the UK to be inadequate to drive productivity growth and close the productivity gap with key competitors. They identify three factors which explain the persistently low productivity for UK companies and the low level of innovation of the UK economy: (1) insufficient investment in capital assets and innovation, (2) positioning on low input cost rather than high value, and (3) inadequate adoption of modern management techniques (Department of Trade and Industry and Economic and Social Research Council, 2003).

Between 1976 and 1979, innovation has contributed to around 50% of total productivity growth in the UK (Geroski, 1989). In particular, the UK firms which have patented their inventions in the US and those which invested in the use of the latest technology (as measured by imports) had a substantial positive effect on productivity (Budd and Hobbis, 1989).

Industry or firm-level studies

In their seminal paper, "Industrial Structure and the Nature of Innovative Activity", Dasgupta and Stiglitz (1980) (Nobel Laureate for Economics) demonstrate a positive relationship between competition and innovation. Competition encourages innovation — as the performance of the companies subject to competition can be compared, they are compelled to improve the cost and functionality of their products and services (Lazear and Rosen, 1981; Nalebuff and Stiglitz, 1983) Competition also raises the demand elasticity for products of competing companies: so that, an innovative company is rewarded by increased sales of its products and services, which in turn enables it to attract more investment and financing at lower cost than less successful companies (Baily and Gersbach, 1995). As higher competition increases risk of failure, managers and workers (especially if there is rent sharing by them) are encouraged to improve efficiency by innovating to ensure survival (Haskel and Sanchis, 1995; Aghion and Howitt, 1998).

In high-tech industries with low concentration — characterised by "creative destruction" — businesses engage in innovative activities to develop differentiated product/services to capture or to maintain market share. This results in intense competition that can reduce rents and lead to some companies going out of business. In contrast, in high-tech industries with high concentration, where a few large firms dominate, technological leadership through innovation — especially when combined with "first-mover advantage" in introducing innovations to market — may confer strong competitive advantage to a company and enable them to earn high rents from their investment in innovation (OECD, 2003).

A positive relationship between competition and innovation has also been confirmed by Aghion *et al.* (2001), Boone and Van Dijk (1998), Porter (1990) and van de Klundert and Smulders (1997). These findings have strongly influenced public- and industrial-policies in many countries (Nickell, 1996).

But, this view of a positive relationship between competition and innovation contrasts with the assumptions inherent in the basic Schumpeterian approach where the opposite is held — that innovation and growth decline with competition, increased competition may reduce innovation (Cohen and Levin, 1989), and the gains from innovation are quickly consumed, lowering the firm's expectations of the rents from innovation, thereby discouraging investment in innovation. This negative relationship between competition and innovation is also supported by other studies showing that companies which have monopoly power and generate supernormal profits — and hence, have less risk of bankruptcy — are better positioned (than companies without monopoly power) to finance innovation activities that enhance their dominant position. This might be especially true if, through internal financing, they can maintain secrecy on technology to further reinforce their dominant position (Kamien and Schwartz, 1982). However, many empirical studies refute these arguments, demonstrating that increased competition does not decrease innovation (Geroski, 1990; Blundell *et al.*, 1999).

R&D plays an important role in a company's productivity (Baily and Chakrabarti, 1985; Georghiou *et al.*, 1986) while innovation positively influences profitability as innovative companies generally have larger market shares, higher profitability and greater resilience in times of economic downturn (Geroski *et al.*, 1993). Innovative companies and those that adopt new technologies enjoy higher profits than companies that are not innovative (Stoneman and Kwon, 1996). As information on product and process innovations diffuse relatively rapidly and as these innovations can be imitated by competitors (Mansfield *et al.*, 1981; Mansfield, 1985), effective IP protection is critical to maintain competitiveness and to recoup costs of innovation.

Earlier studies that analysed benefits of patenting and the ways in which these benefits created incentives for companies to invest in R&D and innovation, produced mixed results (Taylor and Silberston, 1973; Mansfield, 1986; Levin *et al.*, 1987), while other studies argued that rigid patent protection regimes may hinder innovation (Merges and Nelson, 1990; Scotchmer, 1991). But in most contexts patent regimes allow researchers to use IP for research purposes or licence IP from others (Walsh *et al.*, 2003). More recent studies substantiate the value and benefits of IP and patents. Strong IP protection improves chances of success for small companies (Gans and Stern, 2003), enhances their bargaining position when negotiating with larger organisations for licencing or collaboration deals (Grindley and Teece, 1997), and increases their chances of securing financing from investors (Rivette and Kline, 2000). For larger companies, better exploitation and effective management of IP, through in- or out-licencing or defending, can lead to substantial benefits (Kalamas *et al.*, 2002; Hillery, 2004)

The OECD (2005b) report on "Intellectual Property as an Economic Asset", which draws on Kaplan and Norton (2004), highlights the fundamental role IP plays in business performance and economic growth in knowledge-based economies. The report points out that, increasingly, a large proportion of the market value of a company is determined by its intellectual assets — which, as intangible assets, have monetary value and add to the company's balance sheet to increase enterprise value. Indeed, substantial value placed on patents (Gambardella *et al.*, 2005) and patenting innovations significantly increases (up to 47%) the value realised from them (Arora *et al.*, 2003).

Hence, strategic management of IP is important to companies. Yet, many studies show that most companies in knowledge-based economies do not manage their IP strategically or adequately invest in IP generation and management (Arora *et al.*, 2001; Roland Berger Market Research, 2005). This might be because varied valuation techniques produce different values for patents — sending mixed signals to inventors and firms that have invested resources to generate and manage IP (Schankerman and Pakes, 1986; Schankerman, 1998; Hall *et al.*, 2000; Smith and Parr, 2000; Loch and Bode-Greuel, 2001; Harhoff *et al.*, 2004).

Legal protection of the IP rights of the innovators stimulates innovation, as shown by studies demonstrating a positive correlation between the strength of the IP protection and intensity of patenting (OECD, 2005a).

Nonetheless, the relationship between the IP systems, patenting and innovative activity remains complex and the current measures, which focus on investment in R&D, the number of patents filed or granted and the number of citations, are not adequate to capture the extent of innovation activity at firm or national level.

In summary, cross-country, country-level and company-level studies show that innovation, as measured by R&D or patenting, has a positive correlation with economic productivity and enhances market share and profitability at company level. Benefits are best realised when regimes governing intellectual property rights provide incentives for innovation and do not hinder diffusion of knowledge. Empirical evidence also shows that innovation diffuses rapidly to competitor firms and is imitated. Hence, IP protection is important to sustain competitive advantage and allow the creators to capture the benefits of their investment in innovation. Effective management of innovation and IP should be a fundamental strategic objective for countries and companies, particularly in knowledge-based and innovation-intensive economies.

The next section of this paper explores innovation and IP management strategies pursued by countries and companies to enhance competitiveness.

Country Case Studies

Because IP is a powerful lever for economic growth, the role played by governments in shaping IP policy is important. In this section, we analyse differing approaches taken by the US, Japan, China and Europe to promote and manage IP effectively.

The United States

Over the last 25 years, policy makers have played an important role in creating an IP infrastructure in the US. This has encouraged the growth of high-tech industries and created jobs. The "Bayh-Dole Act", which provided a new and uniform way for handling and transfer of federally-funded sponsored research at academic institutions in the US, transformed the parameters within which academia and industry co-operated (USGPO, 1980). By allowing universities to own the IP they created, the act afforded greater freedom for universities to enter into agreements with the private sector, the venture capital industry, and foreign firms and offered substantial rewards to those undertaking successful research. Since the act came into force in 1984, US universities have completed approximately 42,000 licensing deals and have created 4,500 companies. Around 95% of the revenues from these activities come from licencing and 5% from spinouts (Association of University Technology Managers Inc., 1999). Companies with their roots in the US university system now employ hundreds of thousands of people and contribute an estimated $40 billion a year to the country's economy. In particular, the changes that followed Bayh-Dole led to the growth of dynamic companies in the life sciences, IT and defence sectors — where the US now enjoys global dominance.

Since 1980, organisations such as the American Intellectual Property Association, the Intellectual Property Owners, the International Intellectual Property

Alliance, the International Trademark Association and the Anti-Counterfeiting Group, as well as numerous trade associations, have invested significant resources to educate legislators on the crucial role IP plays in the US economy. As a result, a number of legislations to encourage IP have been approved by the US Congress.

In 1982, the creation of the Court of Appeals for the Federal Circuit (CAFC) was also critical to developing a better enabling environment for IP. Based in Washington DC, CAFC is the court of appeal for all US patent cases and ensures consistency in patent litigation. Prior to 1982, appeals were heard by numerous appeals courts for the federal circuit, all with different interpretations of patent law. The consistency brought by the CAFC in enforcing patent laws has provided companies a greater confidence to establish expensive R&D and IP management programs.

Another differentiating aspect of the US IP system is that the Commissioner of the US Patent and Trademark Office is also an under-secretary in the Department of Commerce: a political appointee with power to directly influence IP policy — unlike equivalents in other parts of the world, including Europe and Japan. This has allowed the US to react quickly to technological changes, for example, to modify patent examination guidelines for software and biotechnology sectors.

The US is also a major supporter of the Trade-Related IP Rights Accord adopted by the World Trade Organisation. The protection of IP rights is a major part of all negotiations relating to free trade agreements between the US and other countries.

The US system has created a favourable environment for IP, but a number of issues remain to be addressed. For example, the time taken by the US Patent and Trademarks Office to process patent applications, the quality of the patents granted, and the expense of litigating patents — especially for small companies — are of particular concern. A Patent Reform Act, currently before Congress, is designed to reduce the amount of full scale litigation and address some of these concerns.

Japan

In 2002, Japan's then Prime Minister Junichiro Koizumi convened the Strategic Council on Intellectual Property, composed of individuals drawn from the law, science, industry and academia, to identify ways of improving IP management in Japan. The council proposed action in five key areas: (1) the promotion of IP; (2) greater protection for IP; (3) increased exploitation of IP; (4) an improvement in public awareness of IP issues, and (5) the promotion of IP-related human resources.

Since then, Japan has been engaged in a process of significant IP reform that has seen the creation of the country's first specialist IP court based in Tokyo and the introduction of laws allowing Japanese patent attorneys the same representative rights in court as those enjoyed by lawyers — all at a time when Japanese companies are increasingly likely to view litigation as an acceptable way of solving disputes.

Meanwhile, the Japanese Patent Office (JPO) has been given the task of improving the efficiency of the patent examination system — especially to speed up the application process and to reduce the costs involved. The JPO has also initiated a major education programme, designed to explain the benefits of IP to the country's businesses and to generate a significant upswing in the amount of licensing deals done in Japan. The Customs Law has been amended, so that goods entering the country that infringe Japanese patents can now be seized — a move greatly welcomed by the business sector.

Measures have been designed to incentivise the creation and commercialisation of IP at Japan's universities. Academic institutions now have a brief that encompasses not only education and research but also requires them to make a contribution to society. Since April 2004, all national universities have become corporations, with a reduction in the amount of funding received from the central government. However, it is now much easier for universities to keep the proceeds derived from any IP they create and successfully commercialise. This has resulted in the formation of nearly 40 university technology licensing offices in the country, although to date, the amount of revenue generated from university-created IP remains small.

Ex-prime Minister Koizumi who was actively involved in the rollout of the IP Strategy, has frequently stated that he wanted Japan to be an "IP nation" and — recognising that traditional Japanese manufacturing industries will increasingly struggle to compete with low-wage competition from other Asian countries, notably China, a focus on creating world class IP will enable Japanese companies to maintain a cutting edge. His Cabinet Office had overall responsibility to oversee the reform process and to coordinate government in issues related to IP.

China

China is arguably on the verge of becoming a major technology and IP generator. It will create a significant number of important patents in the next decade, which will enable China to dominate significant technology areas. This stems from the recognition inside China (largely missed by foreign observers) of the fundamental importance of IP to economic growth as well as the natural creativity and inventiveness of the Chinese as a nation.

Most foreign observers look at the still imperfect state of patent enforcement and miss the profound changes that have taken place in China over the last 20 years. To understand this, take the three components of an effective IP regime: (1) the underpinning law, (2) the cost and quality of the patent "right" acquired, and (3) the effectiveness and cost of enforcing that right.

In the mid 1980s, China introduced its first patent and other IP laws to become compliant with the international Berne and Paris IP Treaties. Since then it has passed further updating laws so that, today, China's IP laws are acknowledged to be among the best in the world. IP "rights" for foreigners are generally of high quality and reasonable cost. Patents issued to foreigners by the Chinese Patent Office have been well assessed by their best patent examiners and the 20-year lifetime cost of a Chinese patent is 10% of the total cost of patents for the G8 countries. However, patents issued to Chinese inventors are not always as critically examined.

Although problems remain, the third area, enforcement, has improved enormously and continues to improve. The manufacture of counterfeit drugs is a particular problem, and enforcing IP rights can still be challenging. However, it is possible now to get a patent enforced through the Chinese court system, and this is not costly compared to Europe and the US. In 2004, there was more patent litigation cases filed in China (2550) than in any other country, including the USA. Over 95% of these litigation cases involved only Chinese parties. Chinese companies today are acting as though their IP is important and worth defending. Several of the major pharmaceutical companies have successfully litigated against products that have infringed their patents. But, the quality of the first level courts remains variable, and the relatively independent provincial governments do not always recognise that their courts need to be impartial between foreign and Chinese litigants. The Chinese government appears to be aware of the unresolved problems and willing to address them, for example, by actively encouraging foreign firms to use the recently-created "IP Tribunal of the Supreme Court", whose decisions have been of good quality.

Broader understanding of IP in China has passed a tipping point over the past two years. Chinese companies and universities have begun to understand the international system, its rules and benefits. Acquisition by SAIC of Rover Group's IP — and only the IP — is an indicator of some Chinese companies' sophistication. Chinese companies and universities have begun to realise that if they can invent the next generation of high definition television or mobile phone, they can set the *de facto* global standard. Having also patented these technologies globally, they can then decide to whom to license them. Domestic patent applications are growing at 25–40% a year. Chinese universities now file about as many patents in China (about 6,000 a year) as US universities do in the US. This is six times the number filed in the UK by British universities. The effect of these patents will become visible as technologies mature — ranging perhaps from 5 years in the case of high technology to 15 for pharmaceuticals.

The European Union

Unlike Japan and the US, Europe has not been able to create a strong and user friendly patent infrastructure at reasonable cost for its businesses. It has also failed to create an environment which adequately rewards IP, allowing adequate return on investment.

The IP environment in the EU, a collection of sovereign states, is necessarily complicated. Although there is a European Patent Office (EPO) with headquarters in Munich, the Office does not issue patents that are enforceable across Europe. Instead, an applicant nominates those countries in which it wants to be protected, and, if the application is granted, the EPO will effectively grant national patent rights for each of those countries. The patents granted in this process generally have been well examined and are of a high quality, although the time to grant remains significantly longer than the US or Japan. The patent can also be opposed, or challenged, for a period after grant which provides a further opportunity to weed out questionable patents. However, the fragmented nature of patents in Europe creates two major problems: first, securing EU-wide coverage is significantly more expensive than getting IP protection in the US or Japan (largely from translation costs); and second, there is inconsistency in decisions on IP cases in different countries. These problems weigh most heavily on SMEs or companies in fast moving industries rather than the large companies in the longer lead-time industries such as pharmaceuticals. Also, for the latter industry the length of time for data exclusivity for approved products in the EU is quite beneficial.

As IP law and policy is now framed at the European level, individual countries are not able to decide IP agendas. All decisions have to be reached either by majority or unanimous vote of member states while for directives — which must be incorporated into national laws — approval of the European Parliament is needed. Not surprisingly, 5 years of negotiations for a "Community Patent", originally proposed as an inexpensive, one-stop right designed to cover the entire territory of the EU, have failed. Similarly, the London Agreement on Translations and the European Patent Litigation Agreements (EPLA) — alternatives designed to reduce the cost of patenting in the EU and increase consistency of litigation in participating countries — have stalled for years, although recent initiatives may lead to progress. But, ii is of concern that in 2004 the Commission introduced a Technology Transfer Block Exemption Regulation with virtually no discussion or research exploring its potentially adverse impact on a complex but commercially vital area for the EU.

Unlike the US and China, business method patents are not permitted in Europe, adversely impacting on the ability of European firms to compete with these two countries.

In Europe, two other factors have hindered further development of an enabling environment for IP. First, a vocal and well-organised anti-patent lobby has successfully influenced the debate in matters relating to biotechnology and computer implemented inventions, so that the Computer Implemented Inventions Directive was rejected by the European Parliament, while the Biotechnology Directive has yet to be implemented by member states. Second, patent owners have been ineffective in communicating benefits of IP to key stakeholders — particularly to the politicians who make decisions on the patent laws. Consequently, in contrast to Japan and the US, the EU lacks the high-level political advocates for IP. It is not surprising, therefore, that bold statements on the importance of IP to European competitiveness have yet to be translated to substantive action to create a strong IP infrastructure.

But, some EU countries, such as the UK, have recognised the serious challenges of competing with countries such as China and India, which offer low-cost environments for business. The UK has embraced a multifaceted strategy to compete on "unique value and innovation" with the involvement of businesses, investors, universities and the government to create an environment where innovation can thrive and IP is valued (Department of Trade and Industry, 2003). As with the UK, Germany and the Nordic Countries demonstrate good practice, but these are the exceptions rather than the rule. In most other EU countries, policies that encourage innovation and protect IP are poorly executed or not implemented. Consequently, the extent of patent enforcement and the intensity with which IP rights are protected widely vary in the EU — with substantial weaknesses in several member states that need to be addressed.

For the life sciences industry — where IP generation, development and commercialisation are particularly expensive and risky — weak IP infrastructure is coupled with a reward systems through reimbursement which remains unfavourable, as the EU increasingly relies on cost-containment regimes that do not adequately take into account the risks and expense involved in innovation. Further, in this sector, there are no linkages between the registering authorities which licence new pharmaceutical products and the patent office: hence, creating opportunity for infringement of IP rights.

Company Case Studies

Many companies have developed successful IP management strategies designed to enhance competitiveness and generate higher revenues. We describe below some of these approaches.

IBM

IBM learned about IP the hard way in the late 1980s, when it developed high temperature super-conductors but applied for patents 10 months after its research findings had been published. This led to IBM losing patent protection beyond the US, but also gave its competitors the critical intelligence and the time to replicate the work and to file patents to cover their own developments.

During the 1990s, however, IBM adopted a strategic approach to manage its IP portfolio. Rather than using it as a defensive barrier to prevent rivals encroaching on its territory, IBM began to license out its patents and technology to those that would pay a licence fee. Almost all IBM patents are now available for non-exclusive licence. This critical shift from "closed- to open-innovation" model led to a substantial increase in revenues from licensing activities: from $30 million in 1990 to over $1 billion annually.

IBM has also responded to the challenges posed by the open source community, by announcing in 2005, that it would give individuals, groups, communities and companies working on open-source software free and unfettered access to innovations covered by 500 of its software patents; but, with the condition that open-source software for which the patents are used must meet the Open Source Initiative definition of open-source software.

The central importance IBM attaches to IP management is evidenced by the seniority of the managers responsible for IP (the vice-president for IP and Standards, and the senior vice-president of Technology and Intellectual Property) and the 2005 appointment as the vice-president of IP Strategy of Kevin Rivette, co-author of the well-known book *Rembrandts in the Attic* on IP commercialisation.

Cambridge Display Technology Limited

The British company Cambridge Display Technology Limited (CDT) demonstrates how small-and medium-sized companies can strategically manage IP.

CDT is the leading patent holder and developer of technologies based on light emitting polymers (LEP), a separate but related technology to the organic light emitting diode technology pioneered by Kodak and Motorola Corporation in the 1980s and 1990s.

CDT controls a strong patent portfolio of over 130 patents on materials, electronics, device architectures and manufacturing processes related to LEP technology, complimented by a world-class know-how and a state-of-the-art manufacturing process in these areas — including high-precision ink jet printing for the volume manufacture of display devices.

The strength and density of CDT's IP portfolio means that third party manufacturers of LEP materials as well as display manufacturers (such as Philips, Seiko Epson and DuPont), have to license CDT's fundamental patents and pay royalties. CDT has a novel business model in that it uses its knowledge and know-how in materials, device development and manufacturing processes to offer its licensing partners a support structure. This approach leverages position of CDT and increases its standing in sectors traditionally dominated by large multinationals.

In 2004, CDT successfully raised $15 million of debt capital by collateralising its IP portfolio: demonstrating that small companies with top class IP can raise substantial funds to finance business growth.

Dow

During the 1990s, Dow began to closely examine its IP portfolio and rights, judged to be crucial to business success. Dow has established intellectual capital management (ICM) as a key business process to inform existing and new business strategies at the company. Each of Dow's main businesses has its own multifunctional ICM team, led by intellectual capital managers, who are supported by intellectual capital technologists. Intellectual capital managers are responsible for cross-functional teams, comprised of scientists, business people and patent specialists.

With new inventions, the decision to patent lies with the business that created it. However, the intellectual capital manager of that business will explore with other business units to see if the invention has any application in their areas, and, in such cases, these business units can have an input into the way the patent is structured. If a business unit decides to abandon or license out a patent, other businesses can comment before a final decision. This joined up approach to "invention planning" helps ensure resources are not wasted on patenting inventions that may be technically interesting but do not have a commercial application. Intellectual capital managers also collaborate with key decision makers in each business unit to identify the nature of intellectual capital needed to support a particular strategy, establish whether this is present in house, and, in decisions that involve outsourcing, decide where it can best be obtained.

Novo Nordisk

During the 1990s, while attempting to enter the US market for growth hormone and insulin, Novo Nordisk faced a long-running dispute with Genentech that made it realise the intensity of competition in the markets in which it operates and the importance of IP in deterring competitors.

The dispute with Genentech was settled in 1998 when the two companies agreed to a global cross-licensing deal. Critical to ending the dispute was that while Genentech made claims against Novo Nordisk, the latter was able to make claims against Genentech.

Legal disputes are very expensive and disruptive to a company — as they draw upon key human resources. At the very beginning of a research project, Novo Nordisk market intelligence group undertakes extensive patent-related checks to define the "patent landscape" and to avoid "freedom to operate" disputes. Before a project can start, a series of procedures are completed, a patent attorney is assigned to the project, and a task force is established to manage all patent-related issues throughout the project life — including invention-related disclosures and ongoing patent surveillance on a weekly basis. When the research reaches a point where compounds are selected for development, a detailed freedom-to-operate analysis is done by an internal team along with third party experts from outside the company, and a report is produced. This report is challenged by the attorney "shadowing" the research project and a group of senior managers and attorneys from the IP Group, who in turn make a recommendation to senior executives, who then decide whether the project should proceed to the next stage of development.

When a project moves into full-scale development, there is continuous interaction between the patent department, R&D, marketing and product management teams to capture patenting opportunities, for example, new medical indications and unique selling points, helping to differentiate the compound and enhance the potential to extend the product lifecycle of the product.

Conclusions

Empirical evidence demonstrates the value of IP in creating economic growth. Especially in knowledge-based economies, and R&D intensive sectors of the economy, such as the life sciences industries, IP plays a fundamental role in the decisions to invest in innovation.

Investment in patents to create an IP portfolio and strategic management of IP are critically important for firms to develop competitive advantage and realise maximum value from patents. But, a balance needs to be achieved between the size of an IP portfolio, and the quality, robustness and density (interrelatedness) of the patents it contains.

In addition to enhancing productivity and profitability, IP and patents have a monetary value, which as intangible assets add to a company's balance sheet and increase enterprise value. Evidence suggests that some companies, especially in the US, are using IP creatively, but there is much room to enhance effective management of IP portfolios.

At a country level, the US has approached IP strategically with high level political input and created an IP infrastructure that underpins IP creation and protection. As a result, effective management of intellectual assets is a key building block for US economic policy.

In Japan, the establishment of the Strategic Council on Intellectual Property and subsequent reforms lead by the former Prime Minister Koizumi indicate strong support to develop Japan as an "IP nation".

Major shifts have been taking place in China over the last twenty years and increasingly rapidly in the last few years. China now has an increasingly well-developed IP system and the Government is aware of its shortcomings and is willing to address them.

In the EU, the picture is less encouraging. Although EU patents granted by EPO are of good quality, the patent system itself remains fragmented, slow and expensive, creating particular problems for SMEs or fast moving industries. Patent protection and enforcement of IP rights are inadequate in some member states. There is no EU-wide community patent and this unfavourable environment constrains reward opportunities and acts as a major deterrent to investment decisions as regards innovation.

Political and public understanding of the importance of IP remains poor. Patenting and IP are often trivialised and in many quarters ideological opposition to IP remain strong. While the UK, Germany and the Nordic Countries demonstrate good practice, with initiatives to encourage R&D, innovation and IP management, these are the exceptions rather than the rule. Instead, EU remains home to a heterogeneous mosaic of many member countries, with a lack of senior political figures to champion necessary reforms to create a more enabling environment that encourages innovation and creation of IP.

Progress has been poor in implementing The Lisbon Agenda, which explicitly identified the EU's objective to become the world's leading knowledge-based economy. The life sciences industry is one of the few industries where the EU enjoyed global competitive advantage but this advantage continues to erode. The EU is failing to leverage its knowledge base and infrastructure in the life sciences sectors — and, the ability to leverage this knowledge base is hindered by the cumbersome patent system.

There is a need for substantial investment to encourage more R&D and innovation and to raise awareness of IP amongst the politicians, companies, R&D intensive organisations and the general public in order to clarify any misunderstandings and to communicate the benefits of IP. But this investment needs to be coupled with a system that encourages development and commercialisation of research outputs along with appropriate incentive systems to reward organisations investing substantial resources into development and commercialisation of new technologies. Without this investment coupled with strong political leadership the European dream of becoming the leading knowledge-based economy will remain just that: a dream.

References

Aghion, P *et al.* (2001). Competition, imitation and growth with step-by-step innovation. *Review of Economic Studies*, 68(3), 467–492.

Aghion, P and P Howitt (1998). *Endogenous Growth Theory*. Cambridge, MA: MIT Press.

Arora, A, M Ceccagnoli and WM Cohen (2003). R&D and the patent premium. NBER Working Papers # 9431.

Arora, A, A Fosfuri and A Gambardella (2001). *Markets for Technology: The Economics of Innovation and Corporate Strategy*. Cambridge, MA: MIT Press.

Association of University Technology Managers Inc. (1999). AUTM Licensing Survey: Fiscal Year 1999. Northbrook, IL.

Baily, MN and AK Chakrabarti (1985). Innovation and productivity in United-States industry. *Brookings Papers on Economic Activity*, 2, 609–639.

Baily, MN and H Gersbach (1995). Efficiency in manufacturing and the need for global competition. *Brookings Papers on Economic Activity*.

Blundell, R, R Griffith and J Van Reenen (1999). Market share, market value and innovation in a panel of British manufacturing firms. *Review of Economic Studies*, 66(3), 529–554.

Boone, J and T Van Dijk (1998). Competition and innovation. *Economist-Netherlands*, 146(3), 445–461.

Budd, A and S Hobbis (1989). Cointegration, technology and the long-run production function. Centre for Economic Forecasting Discussion Paper no.10-89, London Business School, London.

Cohen, WM and RC Levin (1989). Empirical studies of innovation and market structure. In *Handbook of Industrial Organization*, R Schlamensee and R Willig (eds.). Elsevier.

Commission of the European Communities (2002). Communication from the commission: More research for Europe. Towards 3% of GDP. Accessible at: http://europa.eu.int/eur-lex/en/com/cnc/2002/com2002_0499en01.pdf.

Dasgupta, P and J Stiglitz (1980). Industrial-structure and the nature of innovative activity. *Economic Journal*, 90(358), 266–293.

Department of Health (2006). Pharmaceutical Industry Competitiveness Task Force. http://www.dh.gov.uk/assetRoot/04/05/83/90/04058390.pdf.

Department of Trade and Industry (2003). Innovation Report. Competing in the global economy: The innovation challenge. London.

Department of Trade and Industry and Economic and Social Research Council (2003). UK Competitiveness: Moving to the Next Stage. http://www.dti.gov.uk/economics/paper3-porter-ketels.pdf.

Gambardella, A, D Harhoff and B Verspagen (2005). The value of patents. http://www.nber.org/~confer/2005/si2005/prl/gambardella.pdf.

Gans, JS and S Stern (2003). The product market and the market for "ideas": Commercialization strategies for technology entrepreneurs. *Research Policy*, 32(2), 333–350.

Georghiou, L, S Metcalf, M Gibbons, T Ray and J Evans (1986). *Post-Innovation Performance*. London: MacMillan.

Geroski, P (1989). Entry, innovation and productivity growth. *Review of Economics and Statistics*, 71(4), 572–576.

Geroski, P (1990). Innovation, technological opportunity, and market structure. *Oxford Economics Papers*, 42(3), 586–602.

Geroski, P, S Machin and J Vanreenen (1993). The profitability of innovating firms. *RAND Journal of Economics*, 24(2), 198–211.

Griliches, Z (1980). Returns to R&D expenditures in the private sector. In *New Developments in Productivity Measurement*, KW Kendrick and B Vaccara (eds.). Chicago: University Press.

Grindley, PC and DJ Teece (1997). Managing intellectual capital: licensing and cross-licensing in semiconductors and electronics. *California Management Review*, 39(2).

Hall, BH, A Jaffe and M Trajtenberg (2000). Market value and patent citations: a first look. NBER Working Paper # 7741.

Harhoff, D, FM Scherer and K Vopel (2004). Citations, family size, opposition and the value of patent rights (vol 32, pg 1343, 2003). *Research Policy*, 33(2), 363–364.

Haskel, J and A Sanchis (1995). Privatisation and X-inefficiency: a bargaining approach. *Journal of Industrial Economics*, 43(3), 301–321.

Her Majesty's Treasury (2003). Lambert review of business university collaboration. http://www.hmtreasury.gov.uk/consultations_and_legislation/lambert/consult_lambert_index.cfm.

Hillery, JS (2004). *Securitization of Intellectual Property: Recent Trends from the United States*. Bethesda: Washington Core.

Intellectual Asset Magazine and European Patent Office (2005). Patents in Europe: helping business to compete in the global economy. Intellectual Asset Management Magazine in Association with European Patent Office, London.

Kalamas, J, GS Pinkus and K Sachs (2002). The new math for drug licensing. *The McKinsey Quarterly*, 4, 9–12.

Kamien, MI and NL Schwartz (1982). *Market Structure and Innovation*. Cambridge: Cambridge University Press.

Kaplan, RS and DP Norton (2004). *Strategy Maps: Converting Intangible Assets into Tangible Outcomes*. Boston, MA: Harvard Business School Press.

Lazear, EP and S Rosen (1981). Rank-order tournaments as optimum labor contracts. *Journal of Political Economy*, 89(5), 841–864.

Levin, RC et al. (1987). Appropriating the returns from industrial- research and development. *Brookings Papers on Economic Activity*, 3, 783–831.

Loch, CH and K Bode-Greuel (2001). Evaluating growth options as sources of value for pharmaceutical research projects. *R&D Management*, 31(2), 231–248.

Mansfield, E (1980). Basic research and productivity increase in manufacturing. *American Economic Review*, 70(5), 863–873.

Mansfield, E (1985). How rapidly does new industrial-technology leak out. *Journal of Industrial Economics*, 34(2), 217–223.

Mansfield, E (1986). Patents and innovation: an empirical study. *Management Science*, 32(2), 173–181.

Mansfield, E, M Schwartz and S Wagner (1981). Imitation costs and patents: an empirical study. *Economic Journal*, 91(364), 907–918.

Merges, RP and RR Nelson (1990). On the complex economics of patent scope. *Columbia Law Review*, 90(4), 839–916.

Nalebuff, BJ and JE Stiglitz (1983). Information, competition, and markets. *American Economic Review*, 73(2), 278–283.

Nickell, SJ (1996). Competition and corporate performance. *Journal of Political Economy*, 104(4), 724–746.

OECD (1998). *21st Century Technologies: Promises and Perils of a Dynamic Future*. Paris: OECD.

OECD (2003). *The Sources of Economic Growth in the OECD Countries*. Paris: OECD.

OECD (2005a). *Innovation Policies: Innovation in the Business Sector*. Paris: OECD.

OECD (2005b). Intellectual property as an economic asset: key issues in valuation and exploitation. *Background and Issues*. Paris: OECD.

OECD (2005c). The new economy: beyond the hype. *Final Report on the OECD Growth Project. Executive Summary*. Paris: OECD.

Porter, M (1990). *The Competitive Advantage of Nations*. New York: MacMillan.

Rivette, KG and D Kline (2000). *Rembrandts in the Attic: Unlocking the Hidden Value of Patents*. Boston, MA: Harvard Business School Press.

Roland Berger Market Research (2005). Applicant panel survey 200, of intentions for filing patent applications at the European patent office and other offices. http://www.european-patent-office.org/aps/2004/main_report04.pdf.

Schankerman, M (1998). How valuable is patent protection? Estimates by technology field. *RAND Journal of Economics*, 29(1), 77–107.

Schankerman, M and A Pakes (1986). Estimates of the value of patent rights in European-countries during the post-1950 period. *Economic Journal*, 96(384), 1052–1076.

Scherer, FM (1982). Inter-industry technology flows and productivity growth. *Review of Economics and Statistics*, 64(4), 627–634.

Scotchmer, S (1991). Standing on the shoulders of giants — Cumulative research and the patent-law. *Journal of Economic Perspectives*, 5(1), 29–41.

Smith, GV and RL Parr (2000). *Valuation of Intellectual Property and Intangible Assets*. New York: John Wiley & Sons.

Solow, R (1957). A contribution to the theory of growth. *Quarterly Journal of Economics*, 70(1), 65–94.

Stoneman, P and MJ Kwon (1996). Technology adoption and first profitability. *Economic Journal*, 106(437), 952–962.

Taylor, CT and ZA Silberston (1973). *The Economic Impact of the Patent System: A Study of the British Experience*. Cambridge: Cambridge University Press.

USGPO (1980). *Patent and Trademark Law Amendments of 1980*. Washington DC: United States Congress, Committee on Government Operations, Legislation and National Security Subcommittee.

van de Klundert, T and S Smulders (1997). Growth, competition and welfare. *Scandinavian Journal of Economics*, 99(1), 99–118.

Walsh, JP, A Arora and WM Cohen (2003). Effects of research tool patents and licensing on biomedical innovation. In *Patents in the Knowledge-Based Economy*, WM Cohen (eds.). Washington, DC: The National Academy Press.

World Intellectual Property Institute (2006). *About Intellectual Property*. Accessible at: http://www.wipo.int/about-ip/en/.

UPTAKE AND DIFFUSION OF PHARMACEUTICAL INNOVATIONS IN HEALTH SYSTEMS

RIFAT A. ATUN* and IPEK GUROL-URGANCI[†]

Centre for Health Management
Tanaka Business School, Imperial College London
South Kensington Campus, London, SW7 2AZ, UK
*r.atun@imperial.ac.uk
[†]i.gurol@imperial.ac.uk

DESMOND SHERIDAN

Department of National Heart and Lung Institute
Imperial College London and St Mary's Hospital, Norfolk Place
London, W2 1PG, UK
d.sheridan@imperial.ac.uk

Multiple interacting factors influence the uptake and diffusion of medicines which are critical to improving health. However, there is a gap in our knowledge on how regulatory policies and other national health systems attributes combine to impact on the utilisation of innovative drugs, and health system goals and objectives.

Our review demonstrates that strong regulation adversely affects access to innovation, reduces incentives for research-based firms to develop innovative products and leads to short- and long-term welfare losses. Short-term efficiency gains from reducing pharmaceutical expenditures may actually increase total healthcare costs, reduce user choice, and in some cases, adversely affect health outcomes.

Decision makers need to adopt a holistic approach to policy making, and consider potential impact of regulations on the uptake and diffusion of innovations, innovation systems and health system goals.

Keywords: Diffusion of innovation; pharmaceuticals; regulatory environment.

Introduction

Sustained improvements in health depend on uptake and diffusion of innovative technologies (Cutler, and McClellan, 2001). The World Health Organization estimates that half of all the gains in global health between 1952 and 1992 resulted from access to better medicines, diagnostics and application of new knowledge.

Remaining gains were due to income improvements and better education (World Health Organization, 1999).

Given the importance of innovations to sustained improvements in health, governments should create a favourable environment for innovation. Creation of such an environment depends on a sound understanding of the innovation process, factors which encourage or hinder innovation, but also the goals and objectives of health systems. Partial understanding of the innovation process, the factors which influence the uptake and diffusion of innovations, and the goals and objectives of health systems may lead to development of policies and regulations which hinder the innovation process as well as the uptake and diffusion of innovations.

This paper provides an overview of innovation models, how these have evolved over time and the consequences of partial understanding of the innovation process. We describe health systems goals and objectives and argue why it is important to understand these when formulating regulatory interventions. We present a summary of a systematic review of empirical studies which explore how broad- and health-system-specific regulations influence the adoption and diffusion of innovative technologies (in this case innovative medicines) in health systems. The paper concludes with a discussion of the findings and policy implications of these.

Innovation Models

In his review of innovation models, Tidd (2000) notes the shortcomings of early models of innovation which consider the innovation process to be linear: driven by "technology push" (a sequence of related R&D initiatives which led to development of a new product or process and eventual adoption in the market place) or "market pull" (when solutions are generated in response a market signal that a new intervention is needed to address a problem). However, these linear "pull" and "push" models do not adequately capture the nature of the innovation process and the innovation ecosystems within which these innovations occur.

However, more recent models of innovation look at the innovation process as a whole and identify that the innovation process is dynamic, discontinuous, incremental, inter-dependent and highly influenced by a number of factors—such as network of actors, availability of resources, incentive systems and constraints. Using these more recent models and viewing innovation from a more holistic lens, it is possible to see how policies based on a partial view of the innovation process can adversely effect innovation. For example, a partial view that focuses on "technology push" alone may encourage investments in R&D that lead to outputs not valued (or needed) by users. On the other hand, a partial view that focuses on the "demand pull" alone may lead to development of products or services that the market wants but risks detachment from technological development, with consequent risks of erosion of competitiveness and technological leapfrogging. Focusing on the "pull" and "push" interaction alone may result in undue emphasis on the early stages of the innovation and an R&D base which has difficulty in translating new discoveries into applicable therapies, as development of reward systems which encourages adoption and diffusion of innovations may be overlooked. Creation of an enabling environment which encourages adoption and diffusion of innovations is critically important to ensure innovators are appropriately rewarded.

A further problem with the predominant innovation models is that they tend to be "generic" rather than domain focused. The innovation process in life sciences, and particularly in the biopharma sector, has a number of distinctive features that is unique to this knowledge-intensive domain. For example, the biopharma sector is characterised by lengthy product life cycles (on average it takes 12 years of R&D before a new chemical entity (NCEs) is launched to market), high-risk due to high attrition rate in R&D (on average only one in 100 NCEs that go into development make it to market), high development costs (estimated to be over US$800 million for a product (DiMasi *et al.*, 2003)), high levels of government regulation, multiple stakeholders involved in decision making, and market failure when regulation is inappropriate or "partial". Another important feature of the innovation process in the biopharma sector is the "bench-to-bedside" interaction. The ability of physicians to work across a wide range of scientific fields at "the bench and bedside" enables continuous innovation, as new technologies and solutions are developed incrementally over many years during which effects of existing innovations on health status of users are observed and solutions incrementally enhanced to address the problems identified (Sheridan, 2006). Understanding these unique features of the innovation process in the life sciences and biopharma sector is therefore critically important.

Health Systems Goals and Objectives

The goals of health systems are to improve the level and distribution of good health, to provide an adequate level of financial risk protection, and to ensure users are satisfied with the services they receive. Health systems should deliver effective services and technologies in an efficient manner, but also be equitable and responsive to user needs. Equity, efficiency, effectiveness and choice objectives all must be balanced to reflect society's preferences and priorities. These priorities will differ in different countries as societal preferences and value systems vary. For instance, the United States, with a more libertarian orientation, emphasises individual choice while in many European countries equity is an overarching societal objective. In order to achieve these health system goals and objectives, governments should encourage the adoption and diffusion of health-improving innovations and mechanisms which efficiently allocate resources to the most cost-effective interventions.

A health system is composed of interacting elements that include: (1) "financing" (how the funds are collected and pooled); (2) "resource allocation and provider payment systems" (how the pooled funds and other available resources, such as human resources, capital investment or equipment, are allocated, and the mechanisms and methods used for paying health service providers); (3) "stewardship and organisational arrangements", which describe the policy- and regulatory-environment, and the structural arrangements for purchasers, providers and market regulators; and (4), "service provision", services the health sector provides as distinct from the structures within which these services are provided (Atun *et al.*, 2007a). Policy makers manage these elements through regulations and incentives to achieve health system objectives and goals. These elements interact, so that changes in one element influence the functioning of others, creating a complex dynamic system. This interaction affects the way the rules, norms and enforcement mechanisms are implemented to generate system responses. As with the behaviour of other complex systems, these responses may not be easy to predict and may indeed be counterintuitive (Atun *et al.*, 2005) — sometimes leading to the opposite effect to the change that was intended. For example, a regulatory intervention aimed at rationing novel technologies or services to reduce costs and improve efficiency may adversely affect equity or effectiveness and indeed increase overall cost of the health system, if a reduction in service- or technology-access in one part of the system causes increased utilisation of services in other parts. Hence, there is a need for more holistic approaches to policy making, with careful examination of possible impact of regulatory interventions on system objectives (Atun and Menabde, 2007).

How Regulation Influences Uptake and Diffusion of Innovations in Health Systems

The influence of regulation on the uptake and diffusion of innovations can be explored through a prism of new innovative drugs. In the pharmaceutical sector, an innovation is defined as a technological advance leading to the creation of a new drug or one that enhances the therapeutic value of an existing drug (Wilsdon and Nitsche, 2004). Diffusion occurs when "an innovation is communicated through certain channels over time among the members of a social system" (Rogers, 2005).

Earlier reviews which have explored diffusion of innovations in service organisations identified that empirical studies in this area were limited in number and narrow in scope, focusing on single factors but not taking into account how broad contextual and health system factors influence the adoption and diffusion process (Greenhalgh *et al.*, 2005). This methodological shortcoming is important because innovations in health systems are influenced by factors such as the compatibility of the innovation with the system, the value added by the innovation in comparison with existing products (Ruof *et al.*, 2002), the institutional or political context within which the innovation is introduced, budgetary constraints, and clinicians' behaviour (Ferlie *et al.*, 2000; Fitzgerald *et al.*, 2003). Building on earlier reviews, we undertook a systematic review of 389 studies which fulfilled our quality criteria for inclusion (from 74,981 published articles identified). These studies explored how the characteristics of an innovation, behaviour of individual and organisational adopters, the communication process (amongst adopters), factors relating to the health system, and factors relating to the broad context influence the adoption and diffusion of innovative medicines.

We analysed how the changes in health system elements (organisational structure, financing, resource allocation, provider payment systems, and service provision) and regulatory changes influence the uptake and diffusion of innovative medicines (Atun *et al.*, 2005). We considered both new molecular entities (drugs with active ingredients that have not already been approved by authorities) and drugs which provide incremental therapeutic advances on active ingredients that have already been approved for market use. These advances might include enhanced compliance, improved safety profiles, and new benefits to patient subgroups. A detailed review and the methodology are described elsewhere (Atun and Gurol-Urganci, 2006).

The Regulatory Environment

An analysis of diffusion patterns of a new therapeutic class of drugs in 15 countries showed developing countries[1] to have lower diffusion speeds than developed countries. Diffusion speeds were positively associated with per capita health expenditure and negatively associated with price levels (Desiraju *et al.*, 2004).

Many countries have introduced cost containment policies for pharmaceuticals (such as reference pricing, limiting number of prescriptions, withdrawing reimbursement, cost sharing, budgetary restrictions, delisting and restrictive drug formularies) to change the behaviour of physicians and patients. These are explored in what follows.

---

[1] As defined by the World Bank, per capita income level less than $9,076. See, Global Economic Prospects and the Developing Countries (2002), The World Bank, Washington, DC.

Price regulation

Direct price controls

Price controls involve setting fixed pharmaceutical prices. New innovative drugs, even those that are first-in-class, are less likely to be introduced in countries with strong price controls, and if launched the market introduction is delayed (Brouwers *et al.*, 2004; Danzon *et al.*, 2005; Kyle 2006a). Firms are less likely to launch their products in other markets following launches in price-controlled markets (Kyle, 2006b). Pharmaceutical price controls reduce incentives for research-based firms to develop innovative products (Calfee, 2000, 2001) and may lead to both short- and long-term welfare losses, the magnitudes of which are affected by the price level set and the price elasticity of demand (Vogel, 2004).

Profit controls

There is limited empirical evidence regarding the effects of profit controls as regulatory mechanisms (Earl-Slater, 1997). Profit controls introduced in Spain in the late 1980s were criticised because they did not lead to reduction in costs and were subsequently abandoned (Darba, 2003). The Pharmaceutical Pricing Regulation Scheme (which sets a maximum profit level for pharmaceutical firms, while allowing them to set launch prices for new medicines) used in the United Kingdom (UK), compared with other approaches has helped reduce the growth of drug expenditures, enabled annual savings in drugs budgets, but also created a stable regulatory environment which encouraged high levels of R&D investment (Burstall, 1997).

Reference pricing

Reference pricing (RP) is designed to work as a cost-containment tool by imposing a maximum reimbursable price to an insured patient for a given class of pharmaceutical products. It affects the pricing behaviour of pharmaceutical firms, which adjust the prices of their branded and generic products in order to preserve access to the reimbursement market, and to protect insured persons from additional out-of-pocket expenses (Ellison *et al.*, 1997; Lopez-Casasnovas and Puig-Junoy, 2000; Pavcnik, 2000). Although many countries have introduced RP schemes over the last two decades, most studies which explore the impact of such schemes are anecdotal and descriptive, while the empirically-based studies on the subject have been criticised for their methodological shortcomings (Puig-Junoy, 2005). Most of the studies published in peer-reviewed journals which explore RP look at narrow measures, such as changes in aggregate expenditure and utilisation, without analysing the impact that these changes on the health status of patients (Schneeweiss *et al.*, 1998).

After RP was first introduced in Germany in 1989, the total number of pre-scriptions initially declined and the market share of generic medicines increased. Expenditure on pharmaceuticals declined due to the changed prescribing behaviour of doctors, lower prices and increased patient charges (Lopez-Casasnovas and Puig-Junoy, 2000). But after this initial decline expenditures began to rise, mainly because of limited impact on prescribing volumes (Giuliani *et al.*, 1998). This pattern con-tinues in Germany today.

In the Netherlands, RP led to an initial price reduction of branded medicines, but the creation of a guaranteed reimbursement ceiling resulted in generic drug pro-ducers increasing their prices to the guaranteed level. Although the market share of generics increased in the 1990s, total savings for the health service were much lower than expected (Koopmanschap and Rutten, 2003). Within one year of introducing RP in Sweden savings were achieved as the average price of drugs affected by the policy declined by 19% and their market share fell 3% (Ljungkvist *et al.*, 1997). However, the entry of new drugs to the market was significantly deterred. This led to higher prices which counterbalanced cost savings achieved (Lundkvist, 2002), and as a result both Norway and Sweden abandoned it (Mrazek and Mossialos, 2004).

In Italy, RP resulted in average decline of 7% in prices (Fattore and Jommi, 1998) and estimated annual savings of 1.6% in total drug expenditures (Rocchi *et al.*, 2004). Adoption of the RP scheme into Andalusia, Spain, failed to achieve the expected consumer price competition (Puig-Junoy, 2004), and savings were less than those realised by other cost-containment policies, such as wholesale- and pharmacist-margin reductions and negative lists (Darba, 2003).

In Europe, savings resulting from RP have fallen far short of the levels expected and this has prompted many European countries to introduce additional cost-containment measures (Dickson and Redwood, 1998).

In 1995, the Canadian province of British Columbia introduced RP for five ther-apeutic classes of drugs. Substitutions with lower-cost alternatives led to initial cost savings; (Hazlet and Blough, 2002; Marshall *et al.*, 2002; Schneeweiss *et al.*, 2002b, 2003; Grootendorst *et al.*, 2005), but the initial rapid fall in the number of prescrip-tions was not sustained (Grootendorst *et al.*, 2001). RP appeared to decrease com-pliance among low-income persons (Schneeweiss *et al.*, 2002b), reduced utilisation of innovative drugs but also reduced outpatient visits by these patients (Hazlet and Blough, 2002). When higher-cost prescriptions were replaced by lower-cost sub-stitutes in one study the rate of physician visits increased, while no changes were observed in the hospital utilisation patterns (Schneeweiss *et al.*, 2003), findings confirmed by another study which found no significant change in health service utilisation or outcomes (Schneeweiss *et al.*, 2002c). In British Columbia, cost sav-ings resulting from RP were attributed to reduced drug utilisation and cost-shifting to patients, rather than to actual changes in drug prices (Schneeweiss *et al.*, 2004).

In Australia and New Zealand, the growth rate of drug expenditures declined (Ioannides-Demos et al., 2002) after the introduction of RP, however the extent to which this can be attributed to RP is difficult to determine as the scheme was accompanied by other regulatory changes in the health system (Lopez-Casasnovas and Puig-Junoy, 2000).

In the US the introduction of RP has been resisted because of fears that it may adversely effect patients (Kanavos and Reinhardt, 2003). Drawing on the experience in Germany, the Netherlands and New Zealand, Danzon and Ketcham concluded that RP in the US Medicare program would disproportionately affect innovative, "on-patent" products, and discourage R&D investment — which over time could disrupt the supply of new innovative drugs and erode US competitiveness in pharmaceuticals (Danzon and Ketcham, 2003).

Cross-country price differentials and parallel trade

Comparison of pharmaceutical prices between countries show drug prices to be higher in Japan than in the US, which in turn are 6–33% higher than the average prices in Canada, Chile, France, Germany, Italy, Mexico, and the UK. It is not just prices that vary. Delayed introduction and low initial-utilisation levels mean that the consumption of innovative medicines in Canada, France, Germany, and the UK is about 50% lower than in the US (Danzon and Furukuwa, 2003).

In the European Union (EU) there is no single market for medicines and price differentials amongst the EU countries have resulted in arbitrage and parallel trade, with leakage of medicines from low-price countries (e.g. Greece) to high-price countries (e.g. UK). In Sweden, within three years of accession, parallel imports accounted for 16% of the sales of top 50 products. On average the prices of drugs subject to competition decreased by 12–19% (Ganslandt and Maskus, 2004) due to market entry of a large number of firms. Most of the profits from parallel trade accrue to "middle-men" rather than to end users or innovators, and this acts to discourage research investment (Kanavos and Costa-Font, 2005). Thus, Szymanski and Valletti (2005) showed that in industries with high R&D investment, parallel trade reduces incentives to invest, and that the positive welfare effects of parallel trade diminish.

Generic entry and price competition

An analysis of seven countries (US, UK, Canada and Germany vs. France, Italy and Japan) confirms that generic price competition is significantly and negatively associated with the degree of regulation in health systems (Danzon and Chao, 2000). In general, entry of generics negatively affects the diffusion of innovative drugs but the extent of impact varies depending on the regulatory environment (Bae, 1997) In less regulated systems such as the US, patent expiry is followed by a rapid market penetration by competing generics and a sharp decline in the price for patented medicines. In systems which administer prices, such as Italy and France, patent expiry results in a more gradual change.

In the US the growth of managed care and regulatory policies which encourage or mandate generic substitution has led to a rapid expansion of the market share of generic drugs (Kane and Saltman, 1997). Similarly, in the UK, selective reimbursement lists, indicative drug budgets, initiatives to change prescribing behaviour and the use of generic names when training medical students, have led to rapid uptake of generics and a decline in the use of off-patent drugs (Burstall, 1997). Increased prescribing of generics was also observed in the Netherlands where a government-led educational campaign targeted physicians to change prescribing patterns (Kanavos and Mossialos, 1999).

Health technology assessment

Health technology assessment (HTA) examines the short- and long-term clinical, economic and social consequences of the application or use of a particular technology (Draborg *et al.*, 2005). HTA uses economic evaluation to assess whether technologies that have been proven safe and efficacious are also cost-effective for the purchaser. This approach, often referred to as a "fourth hurdle" (Freemantle, 1999) is increasingly being used in Europe, North America, Australia and New Zealand to aid priority setting in health systems and to inform reimbursement decisions for new drugs and technologies (Oliver *et al.*, 2004; Hivon *et al.*, 2005).

In the EU economic evaluation studies are being more widely adopted to assess cost-effectiveness of drugs and in deciding whether new drugs should be approved for reimbursement. However, these studies seem to have only a limited and varied influence on decision-making. Thus in England where National Institute for Health and Clinical Excellence (NICE) recommends which of the licenced drugs should be used in the English National Health Service (NHS) and issues guidelines on their use, implementation of these recommendations vary by provider unit and by topic. (Sheldon *et al.*, 2004) Typically, new drugs not approved by NICE are not reimbursed and are not prescribed in the NHS. In contrast, issuance of NICE guidance on use of a new class of medicines and approval by health authorities for reimbursement (Mace and Taylor, 2003) does not guarantee their use in clinical practice.

Changes in Health System Financing

Effect of health insurance

Studies in the US demonstrate that health insurance coverage increases the use of medicines (Leibowitz *et al.*, 1985; Hillman *et al.*, 1999; Lyles and Palumbo,

1999; Danzon and Pauly, 2002; Berndt, 2005). In contrast, lack of insurance coverage restricts access to essential treatment (Blustein, 2000), reduces utilisation of prescription drugs (Cunningham, 2002), and hinders uptake and diffusion of innovations. This is true even where there is demonstrable need and physician awareness of the benefits of the innovative drug (Griffiths *et al.*, 1994). Compared to established participants, new enrolees in an insurance plan utilise more pharmaceuticals, particularly expensive and innovative ones (Stuart *et al.*, 1991; Stuart and Coulson, 1993; Gianfrancesco *et al.*,1994). Medicare enrolees having private prescription drug coverage tend to use newer innovative medicines, compared with enrolees who have no such coverage (Seddon *et al.*, 2001; Lichtenberg, 2002).

Cost sharing

Cost sharing adversely influences the aggregate demand for prescriptions and utilisation of medicines (Layers, 1989; Harris *et al.*, 1990; Hurley, 1991; Ryan and Birch, 1991; Dustan *et al.*, 1992; Huttin, 1994; Gerdtham, 1996; Johnson *et al.*, 1997; Adams, 2001). It also leads to a decline in the utilisation of essential drugs (Stuart, 1998; Fortess *et al.*, 2001; Schneeweiss *et al.*, 2002a), reduces compliance (Dor, 2004), and increases adverse health events (Tamblyn *et al.*, 2001), particularly for poor patients and those with chronic illnesses (Lexchin and Grootendorst, 2004; Stuart and Zacker, 1999). With cost sharing, the decline in utilisation of medicines essential for serious medical conditions is small, as long as out-of-pocket spending is not large (Pilote *et al.*, 2002) and patients' sensitivity to such charges is low (Carrin and Hanvoravongchai, 2003). However, it is unclear from these studies whether cost-sharing has a differential effect on innovative and established drugs.

Drug budgets and prescribing limits

In general, drug budgets adversely affect the uptake and diffusion of innovative medicines by encouraging the use of generic low-cost (rather than cost-effective) drugs (Bradlow and Coulter, 1993; Maxwell *et al.*, 1993; Von der Schulenburg, 1994) and delaying the introduction of new innovative drugs (Le Pen, 2003). Health effects of prescribing changes due to restricted drug budgets have not been adequately studied, but drug budgets do not always lead to cost savings. Indeed, experience suggests that the number of prescriptions or health expenditure may actually increase (Schoffski and Graf von der Schulenburg, 1997; Schwermann *et al.*, 2003), especially if there are no incentives to prescribe efficiently and effectively (McGuire and Litt, 2003).

Restricting or withdrawing reimbursement for drugs leads to reduced prescribing, substitution of newer drugs with older ones, and increased referral of patients to parts of the health system where these drugs may be accessed (Huttin and Andral,

2000). All this has a net result of increased overall prescribing and expenditure (Soumerai, 1990; Ross-Degnan *et al.*, 1993). For example, limiting the number of prescriptions for patients with chronic illness, can lead to a rapid decline in utilisation of medicines, along with an increase in more costly hospitalisations and use of outpatient services (Soumerai *et al.*, 1987, 1991, 1994). However, as the studies examined use changes in aggregate utilisation levels as end points, differential impact of these policies on the uptake of innovative medicines is not clear.

Organisational Changes

A number of studies have explored the impact of new organisational forms on prescribing patterns (changes in the prescribing volume, unit cost of prescribing and prescribing of generic medicines).

General practice fundholding in the UK

General practice (GP) fundholding was introduced in England in 1989 as part of health reforms aimed at improving the efficiency and responsiveness of the health system. These reforms led to a separation of planning and purchasing functions from service provision, but also gave GPs the option to have budgets for management, medicines, and diagnostic tests, and for purchasing services from hospitals. GPs had an economic incentive to use these budgets efficiently, since they could retain savings for investment in their practices.

Given similar budgets for medicines, GP fundholders reduced both the overall annual cost of prescribing (Bradlow and Coulter, 1993) and the rate of increase in prescribing costs more than non-fundholders did (Wilson *et al.*, 1996, 1997). Savings were achieved through a simultaneous reduction in prescribing volume and cost of per item prescribed (Wilson *et al.*, 1995), increased prescribing of generic medicines (Rafferty *et al.*, 1997), and reduced prescribing volume combined with higher unit cost per prescription (Maxwell *et al.*, 1993). Fundholding GPs used therapeutic substitution and therapeutic conservatism to contain prescribing costs. There was no evidence, however, that they were slower than non-fundholding GPs to take up innovative medicines (Wilson *et al.*, 1999). Savings associated with the GP fundholding schemes were observed only in the early years. Within three to four years of joining the scheme, the prescribing patterns of fundholding GPs converged with those of non-fundholding practices (Stewart-Brown *et al.*, 1995; Harris and Scrivener, 1996; Rafferty *et al.*, 1997; Whynes *et al.*, 1997). Changes in prescribing behaviour were observed in non-fundholding GP practices that were given economic incentives and targets to reduce prescribing costs (Bateman *et al.*, 1996).

A major shortcoming of these studies is that none have assessed the impact of fundholding on the quality of prescribing or on the uptake and diffusion of innovative medicines.

Managed care in the US

Managed care (characterised by integrated financing and delivery of services, fixed health care budgets, shift of services from hospitals to ambulatory care, rebates from a manufacturer for inclusion and utilisation of its drugs in the formulary, and a number of mechanisms to control health care costs) was introduced in response to rapidly rising health care costs, and has become the dominant mode of health care financing and delivery in the US.

The overall impact of managed care on cost and utilisation of medicines is mixed (Hurley *et al.*, 1989; Schoenman *et al.*, 1997). But there are no empirical studies which have explored how managed care influences the quality of prescribing relative to innovative medicines, health outcomes and wider economic benefits. Managed care has increased the price elasticity of on-patent medicines (Danzon, 1999). The use these medicines by managed care organisations (MCOs) does not appear to differ from fee-for-service plans, because new innovative medicines satisfy previously unmet needs and are perceived to help reduce total health care costs (even at the cost of some increase in drug expenditure) (Chernew *et al.*, 1997). Furthermore, contracts between MCOs and manufacturers that incorporate discounts and rebates enable the use of innovative medicines (Murray and Deardorff, 1998). With expanded coverage, managed care may lead to increased use of new innovative medicines by improving patient access (Weiner *et al.*, 1991), lowering out-of-pocket payments, and enabling greater use of prescription medicines (Davis *et al.*, 1999).

Service Provision

Medical services cannot be viewed in isolation. Instead, they should be viewed as a network of interrelated activities where interventions in one part of the system result in changes in the use of other parts. Improved access to innovative medicines generally decreases hospitalisation rates and overall health care expenditures.

Disease management

Disease management requires integrated management of chronic illnesses to improve the efficiency, quality and effectiveness of care. This can enhance patient safety, improve health outcomes and achieve economic benefits, provided that it allows appropriate uptake of innovative medicines that help to reduce hospitalisations (Sclar *et al.*, 1994; Armstrong and Langley, 1996).

Formularies

Formularies define a "basket of drugs" for reimbursement, and are used in most countries as a policy tool to control costs and influence demand (Jacobzone, 2005). The effectiveness of formularies in controlling drug costs is not universal, but instead varies by country and therapeutic group (Huskamp, 2003). High degrees of restriction limit access to innovative medicines, increase health care utilisation and decrease incentives for innovation, all without containing costs (Goodwin, 2003) especially over the long-term.

In the US, patients who live in states with closed Medicaid formularies have significantly restricted access to new innovative drugs, including first-in-class drugs (Grabowski, 1988). Conversely, when restrictive formularies are disallowed, access to innovative medicines increases (Walser *et al.*, 1996). For example, in the case of patients who are mentally ill, open access has led to rapid uptake of innovative medicines, and to an increase in drug costs. But overall health expenditure declined due to reduced nursing home use and enhanced equity, as racial disparities in treatment access were eliminated (McCombs *et al.*, 2004). Medicaid's removal of drug formulary restrictions has led to an increase in the number of prescriptions, physician visits, and outpatient visits per person, along with a decline in the number of inpatient hospital admissions (Kozma *et al.*, 1990).

Discussions and Conclusions

Multiple interacting factors influence the uptake and diffusion of drugs, but no studies have yet explored how regulatory and health system elements interact to collectively influence the uptake and diffusion of innovative medicines. A few studies have analysed how particular regulations aimed at containing costs influence prices, utilisation and expenditure of medicines. However the impact of these measures on diffusion of innovative medicines has not been adequately explored. To date, the studies which explored the effect of regulatory interventions on the uptake and diffusion of medicines have relied on aggregate measures, such as volume of medications prescribed and the expenditure for drugs, without analysing the impact on total health expenditures. Further, by focusing exclusively on efficiency, these studies have not adequately explored the impact of regulatory interventions on other health system goals and objectives, such as health outcomes, user satisfaction, effectiveness equity and patient choice. They underscore the dangers of partial understanding of innovation and adverse consequences of regulatory interventions that do not take a holistic view of innovation and health delivery.

Many cost containment policies have consequences beyond drug budgets alone. Strong price regulation adversely affects access to innovation, as innovative medicines are less likely to be launched first in countries that strongly regulate drug prices; it may also lead to welfare losses in the short- and the long-run by reducing incentives for research-based firms to invest in R&D to develop innovative products. RP and restrictive formularies negatively affect the uptake and diffusion of innovative medicines. RP, especially affects diffusion of "on-patent" medicines, by forcing down their prices, thereby diminishing the incentive for research-led firms to invest in R&D. Although RP can achieve short-term savings for drug budgets these savings are not sustained, and health expenditure may actually increase — as many patients whose medicines are switched to lower-cost substitutes because of RP may stop their treatment and experience worsening health outcomes.

HTA is being used more widely in developed countries to aid priority setting and to inform reimbursement decisions for new drugs and technologies. However, few studies have rigorously examined the effect of HTA on the uptake and diffusion of innovations. Long delays during the assessment of new and innovative drugs restrict or excessively delay access to them. As HTA is applied very early in a product's lifecycle, before there is an opportunity to use the drug in the target population, it inadequately captures the benefits offered by those medicines and creates a disadvantage for innovations whose benefits are delayed. This demonstrates the risks of partial understanding of the innovation process in the life sciences, as HTA functions as a cost-containment tool, rather than as a mechanism used to increase adoption and diffusion of effective technologies, reducing opportunities for innovations. A recent pan-European study comparing patient access to cancer drugs concluded that delays in health technology assessments (such those undertaken by NICE) negatively affected patient care by further delaying the availability of licensed new innovative medicines (Wilking and Jonsson, 2005). There are concerns that the recently established Institute for Quality and Efficiency in Medical Care in Germany (Institut für Qualität und Wirtschaftlichkeit im Gesundheitswesen (IQWiG)) may lower the incentives to introduce innovations into the German market and may act as a barrier to uptake of innovative medicines Both IQWiG and NICE require cost-effectiveness analysis before a new innovation is made available to patients (Von der Schulenberg, 2006). This approach has several weaknesses as far as the innovation process is concerned: (1) the true benefit of new drugs is often not apparent until long after their introduction, (2) reliance on limited data from clinical trials and economic models to assess likely cost effectiveness may be misleading, (3) a major element of drug innovation results from clinical experience following the launch of the prototype of a new drug class, which can not be foreseen or predicted, (4) HTA has the potential to impact not only on the diffusion of a particular medicine but also the innovation process and financial mechanisms that generated it as well as potential future innovations that may result from post launch clinical experience of its use. This approach to HTA appears to contradict the main impetus of European science policies which seek to encourage development of a knowledge based economy through research and development and investment in patents (Atun *et al.*, 2007b). It is a unique feature of the life sciences sector in Europe; thus while seeking to promote R&D in this area through Community-supported research programmes, health policies that encourage HTA and cost-containment discourage introduction of new innovative medicines for use (Von der Schulenburg, 2006).

Other policies aimed at cost containment, such as therapeutic substitution and cost sharing can adversely influence diffusion of new medicines and by reducing the demand for necessary drugs, can lead to high levels of adverse health events and higher overall health system costs, because savings achieved from cost-sharing policies may be outstripped by higher outpatient use and greater hospitalisation. In contrast, expansion of health insurance coverage leads to an increase in utilisation of pharmaceuticals. But lack of health insurance and reduced coverage create substantial barriers to the uptake and diffusion of innovative pharmaceuticals, deters use of necessary medicines, and undermines equity. Poorer segments of the population, namely, the elderly and the chronically ill, would disproportionately bear the brunt of these polices.

Although disease management programmes may result in higher pharmaceutical costs, appropriate increase in the uptake of innovative medicines leads to fewer hospitalisations, improved quality of care, and therefore overall cost savings and improved health outcomes.

In conclusion, there are major gaps in the evidence base needed to inform policy on the uptake and diffusion of new medicines. Studies that explore how changes in the regulatory environment and health system elements influence the uptake of drugs are too narrow in scope: most of them focus on narrow efficiency measures (such as aggregate utilisation of drugs or pharmaceutical expenditures), but fail adequately to explore the impact of these changes on the uptake of innovative medicines and innovation systems, as well as other health system objectives such as equity, effectiveness and choice. These narrow approaches reflect a partial understanding of the innovation process in the biopharmaceutical sector and the complexities of translating new knowledge into new medicines.

This review confirms the need for decision makers to adopt a more holistic approach to policy-making and regulation. The potential impact of these policies and regulations on health system goals and objectives should be explored carefully. Decision makers must look beyond narrow efficiency measures in one part of the health system (such as pharmaceutical budgets) and consider the impact of health policies on the health system as a whole and innovation systems in the biopharma sector.

References

Adams, AS (2001). The case for a medicare drug coverage benefit: a critical review of the empirical evidence. *Annual Review of Public Health*, 22, 49–61.

Armstrong, EP and PC Langley (1996). Disease management programs. *American Journal of Health System Pharmacy*, 53(1), 53–58.

Atun, RA and I Gurol-Urganci (2006). Factors influencing the uptake and diffusion of pharmaceutical innovations: a systematic review. Imperial College London, Tanaka Business School Discussion Paper.

Atun, RA and N Menabde (2007). Health systems and systems thinking. In *Health Systems and Communicable Diseases: Challenges to Transitional Societies*, RJ Coker, RA Atun and M McKee (eds.). European Observatory in Health Systems and Open University Press, forthcoming.

Atun, RA *et al.* (2005). Analysis of how the health systems context shapes responses to the control of human immunodeficiency virus: case-studies from the Russian Federation. *Bulletin of the World Health Organization*, 83(10), 730–738.

Atun, RA *et al.* (2007a). Diffusion of complex health innovations—implementation of primary care reforms in Bosnia and Herzegovina: qualitative study. *Health Policy and Planning*, 22(1), 28–39.

Atun, RA *et al.* (2007b). Innovation, patents and economic growth. *International Journal of Innovation Management*, 11(2), 279–297.

Bae, JP (1997). Drug patent expirations and the speed of generic entry. *Health Services Research*, 32(1), 87–101.

Bateman, DN *et al.* (1996). A prescribing incentive scheme for non-fundholding general practices: an observational study. *British Medical Journal*, 313(7056), 535–538.

Berndt, E (2005). The U.S. pharmaceutical industry why major growth in times of cost containment. *Health Affairs*, 20(2), 100–114.

Blustein, J (2000). Drug coverage and drug purchases by medicare beneficiaries with hypertension. *Health Affairs*, 19(2), 219–230.

Bradlow, J and A Coulter (1993). Effect of fundholding and indicative prescribing schemes on general practitioners' prescribing costs. *British Medical Journal*, 307(6913), 1186–1189.

Brouwers, CA, MB Silverstein and T Wolff (2004). Adverse consequences of OECD government interventions in pharmaceutical markets on the U.S. economy and consumer. *BCG White Paper*.

Burstall, ML (1997). The management of the cost and utilisation of pharmaceuticals in the United Kingdom. *Health Policy*, 41 (Suppl), S27–S43.

Calfee, JE (2000). The increasing necessity for market-based pharmaceutical prices. *Pharmacoeconomics*, 18(Suppl 1), 47–57.

Calfee, JE (2001). Pharmaceutical price controls and patient welfare. *Annals of Internal Medicine*, 134(11), 1060–1064.

Carrin, G and P Hanvoravongchai (2003). Provider payments and patient charges as policy tools for cost-containment: how successful are they in high-income countries? *Human Resources for Health*, 1(1).

Chernew, M, AM Fendrick and RA Hirth (1997). Managed care and medical technology: implications for cost growth. *Health Affairs*, 16(2), 196–206.

Cunningham, PJ (2002). Prescription drug access: not just a Medicare problem. *Issue Brief - Center for Studying Health System Change*, 51, 1–4.

Cutler, DM and M McClellan (2001). Is technological change in medicine worth it? *Health Affairs*, 20(5), 11–29.

Danzon, PM (1999). The Pharmaceutical Industry. The Wharton School — University of Pennsylvania.

Danzon, PM and LW Chao (2000). Cross-national price differences for pharmaceuticals: how large, and why? *Journal of Health Economics*, 19(2), 159–195.

Danzon, PM and M Furukuwa (2003). Prices and availability of pharmaceuticals evidence from nine countries. *Health Affairs*, July–December(Suppl), Web Exclusives: W3-521-36.

Danzon, PM and JD Ketcham (2003). Reference pricing of pharmaceuticals for medicare: evidence from Germany, the Netherlands and New Zealand. NBER Working Papers, # 10007.

Danzon, PM and MV Pauly (2002). Health insurance and the growth of pharmaceutical expenditures. *Journal of Law & Economics*, 45, 587–613.

Danzon, PM, RY Wang and L Wang (2005). The impact of price regulation on the launch delay of new drugs: evidence from twenty-five major markets in the 1990s. *Health Economics*, 14, 269–292.

Darba, J (2003). Pharmaceutical expenditure in Spain: evolution and cost containment measures during 1998–2001. *European Journal of Health Economics*, 4(3), 151–157.

Davis, M et al. (1999). Prescription drug coverage, utilization, and spending among Medicare beneficiaries. *Health Affairs*, 18(1), 231–243.

Desiraju, R, H Nair and P Chintagunta (2004). Diffusion of new pharmaceutical drugs in developing and developed nations. *International Journal of Research in Marketing*, 21(4), 341–357.

Dickson, M and H Redwood (1998). Pharmaceutical reference prices: how do they work in practice? *Pharmacoeconomics*, 14(5), 471–479.

DiMasi, J, R Hansen and H Grabowski (2003). The price of innovation new estimates of drug development costs. *Journal of Health Economics*, 22(2), 151–185.

Dor, A (2004). Does cost sharing affect compliance. NBER Working Paper # 10738.

Draborg, E et al. (2005). International comparison of the definition and the practical application of health technology assessment. *International Journal of Technology Assessment in Health Care*, 21(1), 89–95.

Dustan, HP et al. (1992). Report of the task force on the availability of cardiovascular drugs to the medically indigent. *Circulation*, 85(2), 849–860.

Earl-Slater, A (1997). Regulating the price of the UK's drugs: second thoughts after the government's first report. *British Medical Journal*, 314(7077), 365–368.

Ellison, S *et al.* (1997). Characteristics of demand for pharmaceutical products an examination of four cephalosporins. *Rand Journal of Economics*, 28(3), 426–446.

Fattore, G and C Jommi (1998). The new pharmaceutical policy in Italy. *Health Policy*, 46(1), 21–41.

Ferlie, E, L Fitzgerald and M Wood (2000). Getting evidence into clinical practice: an organisational behaviour perspective. *Journal of Health Services Research and Policy*, 5(2), 96–102.

Fitzgerald, L, E Ferlie and C Hawkins (2003). Innovation in healthcare: how does credible evidence influence professionals? *Health & Social Care in the Community*, 11(3), 219–228.

Fortess, EE *et al.* (2001). Utilization of essential medications by vulnerable older people after a drug benefit cap: importance of mental disorders, chronic pain, and practice setting. *Journal of American Geriatric Society*, 49(6), 793–797.

Freemantle, N (1999). Does the UK National Health Service need a fourth hurdle for pharmaceutical reimbursement to encourage the more efficient prescribing of pharmaceuticals? *Health Policy*, 46(3), 255–265.

Ganslandt, M and KE Maskus (2004). Parallel imports and the pricing of pharmaceutical products: evidence from the European Union. *Journal of Health Economics*, 23(5), 1035–1057.

Gerdtham, UG (1996). The impact of user charges on the consumption of drugs: empirical evidence and economic implications. *Pharmacoeconomics*, 9(6), 478–483.

Gianfrancesco, FD, AP Baines and D Richards (1994). Utilization effects of prescription drug benefits in an aging population. *Health Care Financing Review*, 15(3).

Giuliani, G, G Selke and L Garattini (1998). The German experience in reference pricing. *Health Policy*, 44(1), 73–85.

Goodwin, FK (2003). Impact of formularies on clinical innovation. *Journal of Clinical Psychiatry*, 64(Suppl 17), 11–14.

Grabowski, H (1988). Medicaid patients' access to new drugs. *Health Affairs*, 7(5), 102–114.

Greenhalgh, T, G Robert, P Bate, F Macfarlane and O Kyriakidou (2005). *Diffusion of Innovations in Health Service Organisations: A Systematic Literature Review*. Oxford: Blackwell.

Griffiths, RI *et al.* (1994). A review of the first year of medicare coverage of erythropoietin. *Health Care Financing Review*, 15(3), 83–102.

Grootendorst, PV *et al.* (2001). Impact of reference-based pricing of nitrates on the use and costs of anti-anginal drugs. *Canadian Medical Association Journal*, 165(8), 1011–1019.

Grootendorst, PV *et al.* (2005). The impact of reference pricing of nonsteroidal anti-inflammatory agents on the use and costs of analgesic drugs. *Health Services Research*, 40(5 Pt 1), 1297–1317.

Harris, BL, A Stergachis and LD Ried (1990). The effect of drug co-payments on utilization and cost of pharmaceuticals in a health maintenance organization. *Medical Care*, 28(10), 907–917.

Harris, CM and G Scrivener (1996). Fundholders' prescribing costs: the first five years. *British Medical Journal*, 313(7071), 1531–1534.

Hazlet, TK and DK Blough. (2002). Health services utilization with reference drug pricing of histamine(2) receptor antagonists in British Columbia elderly. *Medical Care*, 40(8), 640–649.

Hillman, AL *et al.* (1999). Financial incentives and drug spending in managed care. *Health Affairs*, 18(2), 189–200.

Hivon, M *et al.* (2005). Use of health technology assessment in decision making: corresponsibility of users and producers? *International Journal of Technology Assessment in Health Care*, 21(2), 268–275.

Hurley, J (1991). The effects of co-payments within drug reimbursement programs. *Canadian Public Policy*, 17(4), 473–489.

Hurley, RE, JE Paul and DA Freund (1989). Going into gatekeeping: an empirical assessment. *QRB Quality Review Bulletin*, 15(10), 306–314.

Huskamp, HA (2003). Managing psychotropic drug costs: will formularies work? *Health Affairs*, 22(5), 84–96.

Huttin, C (1994). The use of prescription charges. *Health Policy*, 27(1), 53–73.

Huttin, C and J Andral (2000). How the reimbursement system may influence physicians' decisions results from focus groups interviews in France. *Health Policy*, 54(2), 67–86.

Ioannides-Demos, LL, JE Ibrahim and JJ McNeil (2002). Reference-based pricing schemes: effect on pharmaceutical expenditure, resource utilisation and health outcomes. *Pharmacoeconomics*, 20(9), 577–591.

Jacobzone, S (2005). Pharmaceutical policies in OECD countries: reconciling social and industrial goals. OECD Labour Market and Social Policy Occasional Papers, # 40.

Johnson, RE *et al.* (1997). The impact of increasing patient prescription drug cost sharing on therapeutic classes of drugs received and on the health status of elderly HMO members. *Health Services Research*, 32(1), 103–122.

Kanavos, P and J Costa-Font (2005). Pharmaceutical parallel trade in Europe: stakeholder and competition effects. *Economic Policy*, 20 (44), 753–798.

Kanavos, P and E Mossialos (1999). Outstanding regulatory aspects in the European pharmaceutical market. *Pharmacoeconomics*, 15(6), 519–533.

Kanavos, P and U Reinhardt (2003). Reference pricing for drugs: is it compatible with U.S. health care? *Health Affairs*, 22(3), 16–30.

Kane, NM and RB Saltman (1997). Comparative experience in home care and pharmaceutical policy. *Health Policy*, 41 (Suppl), S1–S7.

Koopmanschap, MA and FF Rutten (2003). The drug budget silo mentality: the Dutch case. *Value in Health*, 6 (Suppl 1), S46–S51.

Kozma, CM, CE Reeder and EW Lingle (1990). Expanding medicaid drug formulary coverage: effects on utilization of related services. *Medical Care*, 28(10), 963–977.

Kyle, M (2006a). Pharmaceutical price controls and entry strategies. *Review of Economics and Statistics*, in press.

Kyle, M (2006b). The role of firm characteristics in pharmaceutical product launches. *RAND Journal of Economics*, in press.

Layers, RJ (1989). Prescription charges, the demand for prescriptions and morbidity. *Applied economics*, 21(8).

Le Pen, C (2003). The drug budget silo mentality: the French case. *Value in Health*, 6 (Suppl 1), S10–S19.

Leibowitz, A, WG Manning and JP Newhouse (1985). The demand for prescription drugs as a function of cost-sharing. *Social Science & Medicine*, 21(10), 1063–1069.

Lexchin, J and P Grootendorst (2004). Effects of prescription drug user fees on drug and health services use and on health status in vulnerable populations: a systematic review of the evidence. *International Journal of Health Services*, 34(1), 101–122.

Lichtenberg, F (2002). Benefits and costs of newer drugs an update. NBER Working Paper No. 8996.

Ljungkvist, MO, D Andersson and B Gunnarsson (1997). Cost and utilisation of pharmaceuticals in Sweden. *Health Policy*, 41(Suppl 1), S55–S69.

Lopez-Casasnovas, G and J Puig-Junoy (2000). Review of the literature on reference pricing. *Health Policy*, 54(2), 87–123.

Lundkvist, J (2002). Pricing and reimbursement of drugs in Sweden. *European Journal of Health Economics*, 3(1), 66–70.

Lyles, A and FB Palumbo (1999). The effect of managed care on prescription drug costs and benefits. *Pharmacoeconomics*, 15(2), 129–140.

Mace, S and D Taylor (2003). Adherence to NICE guidance for the use of anticholinesterases. *Disease Management & Health Outcomes*, 11(2), 129–137.

Marshall, JK *et al.* (2002). Impact of reference-based pricing for histamine-2 receptor antagonists and restricted access for proton pump inhibitors in British Columbia. *Canadian Medical Association Journal*, 166(13), 1655–1662.

Maxwell, M *et al.* (1993). General practice fundholding: observations on prescribing patterns and costs using the defined daily dose method. *British Medical Journal*, 307(6913), 1190–1194.

McCombs, JS, P Mulani and PJ Gibson (2004). Open access to innovative drugs: treatment substitutions or treatment expansion? *Health Care Financing Review*, 25(3), 35–53.

McGuire, A and M Litt (2003). UK budgetary systems and new health-care technologies. *Value in Health*, 6 (Suppl 1), S64–S73.

Mrazek, MF and E Mossialos (2004). Regulating pharmaceutical prices. In *Regulating Pharmaceuticals in Europe: striving for Efficiency, Equity*; E Mossialos, T Walley and MF Mrazek (eds.). London: the European Observatory on Health Systems and Policies, Brussels, and Open University Press.

Murray, MD and FW Deardorff (1998). Does managed care fuel pharmaceutical industry growth? *Pharmacoeconomics*, 14(4), 341–348.

Oliver, A, E Mossialos and R Robinson (2004). Health technology assessment and its influence on health-care priority setting. *International Journal of Technology Assessment in Health Care*, 20(1), 1–10.

Pavcnik, N (2000). Do pharmaceutical prices respond to insurance? NBER Working Papers # 7865.

Pilote, L *et al.* (2002). The effects of cost-sharing on essential drug prescriptions, utilization of medical care and outcomes after acute myocardial infarction in elderly patients. *Canadian Medical Association Journal*, 167(3), 246–252.

Puig-Junoy, J (2004). Incentives and pharmaceutical reimbursement reforms in Spain. *Health Policy*, 67(2), 149–165.

Puig-Junoy, J (2005). What is required to evaluate the impact of pharmaceutical reference pricing? *Applied Health Economics and Health Policy*, 4(2), 87–98.

Rafferty, T, K Wilson-Davis and H McGavock (1997). How has fundholding in Northern Ireland affected prescribing patterns? A longitudinal study. *British Medical Journal*, 315(7101), 166–170.

Rocchi, F, A Addis and N Martini (2004). Current national initiatives about drug policies and cost control in Europe: the Italy example. *Journal of Ambulatory Care Management*, 27(2), 127–131.

Rogers, EM (2005). *Diffusion of Innovations*. New York: Free Press.

Ross-Degnan, D *et al.* (1993). Examining product risk in context: market withdrawal of zomepirac as a case study. *Journal of American Medical Association*, 270(16), 1937–1942.

Ruof, J *et al.* (2002). Diffusion of innovations: treatment of Alzheimer's disease in Germany. *Health Policy*, 60(1), 59–66.

Ryan, M and S Birch (1991). Charging for health care: evidence on the utilisation of NHS prescribed drugs. *Social Science & Medicine*, 33(6), 681–687.

Schneeweiss, S *et al.* (2004). Net health plan savings from reference pricing for angiotensin-converting enzyme inhibitors in elderly British Columbia residents. *Medical Care*, 42(7), 653–660.

Schneeweiss, S, M Maclure and SB Soumerai (2002a). Prescription duration after drug copay changes in older people: methodological aspects. *Journal of American Geriatric Society*, 50(3), 521–525.

Schneeweiss, S, O Schoffski and GW Selke (1998). What is Germany's experience on reference based drug pricing and the etiology of adverse health outcomes or substitution? *Health Policy*, 44(3), 253–260.

Schneeweiss, S *et al.* (2002b). Impact of reference-based pricing for angiotensin-converting enzyme inhibitors on drug utilization. *Canadian Medical Association Journal*, 166(6), 737–745.

Schneeweiss, S *et al.* (2003). Clinical and economic consequences of reference pricing for dihydropyridine calcium channel blockers. *Clinical Pharmacology and Therapeutics*, 74(4), 388–400.

Schneeweiss, S *et al.* (2002c). Outcomes of reference pricing for angiotensin-converting-enzyme inhibitors. *New England Journal of Medicine*, 346(11), 822–829.

Schoenman, JA, WN Evans and CL Schur (1997). Primary care case management for Medicaid recipients: evaluation of the Maryland access to care program. *Inquiry*, 34(2), 155–170.

Schoffski, O and Graf von der Schulenburg JM (1997). Unintended effects of a costcontainment policy: results of a natural experiment in Germany. *Social Science & Medicine*, 45(10), 1537–1539.

Schwermann, T, W Greiner and JM Von der Schulenburg (2003). Using disease management and market reforms to address the adverse economic effects of drug budgets and price and reimbursement regulations in Germany. *Value in Health*, 6 (Suppl 1), S20–S30.

Sclar, DA *et al.* (1994). Antidepressant pharmacotherapy: economic outcomes in a health maintenance organization. *Clinical Therapeutics*, 16(4), 715–730.

Seddon, ME *et al.* (2001). Quality of ambulatory care after myocardial infarction among Medicare patients by type of insurance and region. *American Journal of Medicine*, 111(1), 24–32.

Sheldon, TA *et al.* (2004). What's the evidence that NICE guidance has been implemented? Results from a national evaluation using time series analysis, audit of patients' notes, and interviews. *British Medical Journal*, 329(7473).

Sheridan, D (2006). Development and innovation in cardiovascular medicine. Imperial College London Discussion Paper.

Soumerai, SB (1990). Withdrawing payment for nonscientific drug therapy: intended and unexpected effects of a large-scale natural experiment. *Journal of American Medical Association*, 263(6), 831–839.

Soumerai, SB *et al.* (1987). Payment restrictions for prescription drugs under Medicaid: effects on therapy, cost, and equity. *New England Journal of Medicine*, 317(9), 550–556.

Soumerai, SB *et al.* (1991). Effects of medicaid drug-payment limits on admission to hospitals and nursing homes. *New England Journal of Medicine*, 325(15), 1072–1077.

Soumerai, SB *et al.* (1994). Effects of a limit on Medicaid drugreimbursement benefits on the use of psychotropic agents and acute mental health services by patients with schizophrenia. *New England Journal of Medicine*, 331(10), 650–655.

Stewart-Brown, S *et al.* (1995). The effects of fundholding in general practice on prescribing habits three years after introduction of the scheme. *British Medical Journal*, 311(7019), 1543–1547.

Stuart, B (1998). Ability to pay and the decision to medicate. *Medical Care*, 36(2), 202–211.

Stuart, B *et al.* (1991). Patterns of outpatient prescription drug use among Pennsylvania elderly. *Health Care Financing Review*, 12(3), 61–72.

Stuart, B and NE Coulson (1993). Dynamic aspects of prescription drug use in an elderly population. *Health Services Research*, 28(2), 237–264.

Stuart, B and C Zacker (1999). Who bears the burden of Medicaid drug copayment policies? *Health Affairs*, 18(2), 201–212.

Szymanski, S and T Valletti (2005). Parallel trade, price discrimination, investment and price caps. *Economic Policy*, (44).

Tamblyn, R *et al.* (2001). Adverse events associated with prescription drug cost-sharing among poor and elderly persons. *Journal of American Medical Association*, 285(4), 421–429.

Tidd, J (2000). *From Knowledge Management to Strategic Competence: measuring Technological, Market and Organizational Innovation*. London: Imperial College Press.

Vogel, RJ (2004). Pharmaceutical pricing, price controls, and their effects on pharmaceutical sales and research and development expenditures in the European Union. *Clinical Therapeutics*, 26(8), 1327–1340.

Von der Schulenburg, JM (1994). The German health care system at the crossroads. *Health Economics*, 3(5), 301–303.

Von der Schulenburg, JM (2006). The regulatory environment for pharmaceutical innovation in Europe. Imperial College London Discussion Paper.

Walser, BL, D Ross-Degnan and SB Soumerai (1996). Do open formularies increase access to clinically useful drugs? *Health Affairs*, 15(3), 95–109.

Weiner, JP *et al.* (1991). Impact of managed care on prescription drug use. *Health Affairs*, 10(1), 140–154.

Whynes, DK, T Heron and AJ Avery (1997). Prescribing cost savings by GP fundholders: long-term or short-term? *Health Economics*, 6(2), 209–211.

Wilking, N and B Jonsson (2005). A pan-European comparison regarding patient access to cancer drugs. Karolinska Institute.

Wilsdon, T and R Nitsche (2004). Innovations in the pharmaceutical sector. *Accessible at URL:* http://pharmacos .eudra.org/F2/pharmacos/docs/Doc2004/nov/EU%20Pharma%20Innovatio n_25-11-04.pdf. Charles River Associates ENTR/03/28.

Wilson, RP, I Buchan and T Walley (1995). Alterations in prescribing by general practitioner fundholders: an observational study. *British Medical Journal*, 311(7016), 1347–1350.

Wilson, RP *et al.* (1996). Influences of practice characteristics on prescribing in fundholding and non-fundholding general practices: an observational study. *British Medical Journal*, 313(7057), 595–599.

Wilson, RP *et al.* (1997). General practice fundholders' prescribing savings in one region of the United Kingdom, 1991–1994. *Health Policy*, 42(1), 29–37.

Wilson, RP *et al.* (1999). Therapeutic substitution and therapeutic conservatism as cost-containment strategies in primary care: a study of fundholders and non-fundholders. *British Journal of General Practice*, 49(443), 431–435.

World Health Organization (1999). The World Health Report 1999. WHO.

PARTNERSHIP AND INNOVATION IN THE LIFE SCIENCES

DOMINIQUE KLEYN* and RICHARD KITNEY[†]

Imperial College London, London, UK
*d.kleyn@imperial.ac.uk
[†]*r.i.kitney@imperial.ac.uk*

RIFAT A. ATUN

Department of Centre for Health Management
Tanaka Business School, Imperial College London, London, UK

Government support for partnering between BioPharma companies and universities is growing in the UK and some European countries but few studies have explored these partnerships.

Through interviews and a survey of key institutions we explored perceptions of key informants on industry and university partnerships. Study participants identified that partnering helped them to increase innovation in R&D and led them to adopt more open approaches to innovation.

Organisational structures to coordinate and support partnerships; flexibility in operational management to solve problems in establishing and running these partnerships; leadership, especially by investigators to champion and lead collaborations; developing organisational capabilities of universities; and creation of an enabling environment by governments were identified as the critical success factors for partnering. The challenges faced were identified as lack of funding for university research teams; pressure on pricing from industry partners; disagreements on IP ownership; asymmetry of industry and university capabilities in partnering; and lack of administrative support with excessive bureaucracy from universities.

Keywords: Industry and university partnerships; life sciences; pharmaceuticals and biotechnology; innovation management and open innovation; R&D collaborations; contracting out; outsourcing.

Introduction

The BioPharma sector is underpinned by accumulation of knowledge and new discoveries. To survive and maintain growth, companies must constantly invest in research to develop products based on new technologies and processes — often across broad market sectors. Econometric studies (Bottazzi *et al.*, 2001) show the key drivers of growth in this industry are innovations which create new therapeutic areas and markets and incremental therapeutic improvements which increase competition within existing markets.

In the 1980s, pharmaceutical companies evolved as integrated organisations, managing key activities along the value chain from research to development, manufacturing, marketing, sales and distribution. This was, in part, because few others had the knowledge or the capability to manage and assume the risk of developing new products (Penrose, 1959). In this period, partnerships between pharmaceutical companies and other organisations tended to be based on arm's length arrangements, for example, licensing an invention in return for an upfront payment and royalty on sales. Often, large companies operated a central licensing office to manage such arrangements.

However, in the 1990s the costs of R&D and risks of investment rapidly increased because companies were investing in new technologies and responding to higher regulatory pressures, whilst also having to more rapidly introduce new families of products with additional therapeutic benefits. As a result, pharmaceutical companies began to search for alternative models to the traditional integrated R&D approach in order to enhance their innovative capability and reduce the time and cost of taking new drug targets through the development process. Realising that valuable ideas can come from inside or outside the company, many firms have established structures which allow contracting-out elements of their R&D function to boost R&D productivity (James, 1994; Gambardella *et al.*, 2000; FDA, 2004). In this so-called "Discovery and Distribution" model (Taafe, 1996) BioPharma companies became increasingly more sophisticated in developing collaborations with a range of partners in a particular field or a preferred partner in a specific area. For example, during the 1990s Celltech Biologics supplied specialist fermentation technology for the bulk manufacture of therapeutic monoclonal antibodies to many major pharmaceutical companies (http://www.ucb-group.com/about_ucb/history).

To maintain technological superiority in intensely competitive environments pharmaceutical companies must continually innovate to develop new products or to create new markets for their existing products (Lamoreaux and Sokoloff, 1996). But, as the pace of technological change increases and the scientific knowledge becomes more widely dispersed, even these research-intensive companies need to actively acquire new products from external sources to complement their in-house R&D capability (HITF, 2004). This new model requires new capabilities to shift from closed innovation with a focus on an internal pipeline of products to open innovation which draws on new technologies developed by others (Chesbrough, 2003).

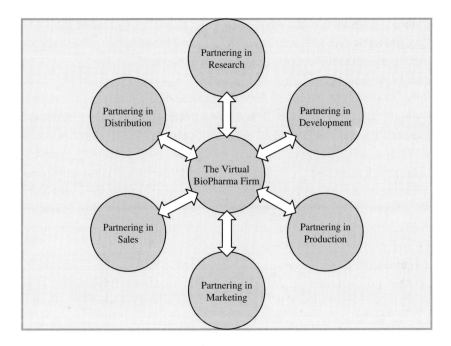

Fig. 1. The Virtual BioPharma Firm.

Collaborations between companies operating in the life sciences space have led to a more flexible organisational model: one which enables companies to focus on one part of the value chain and outsource activities in others. Emerging organisational models for BioPharma companies now range from the traditional integrated R&D approach to more "virtual" models (Fig. 1). In this latter mode the key competence of a company is centred on its ability to find appropriate technologies and partners, and build on its experience of managing expensive, complex and high-risk R&D and commercialization projects—an endeavour that requires large financial outlay and the assumption of substantial market risk. This approach needs strong leadership and significant commitment of senior management time as partnering is a resource intensive process.

Universities have long been an important source of commercially exploitable technology for pharmaceutical companies (Henderson *et al.*, 1994). The universities, in turn, have benefited from an exchange of information and ideas with these companies (Cockburn, I, and R Henderson, 1996). In recent years many universities in the US, some countries in Europe, and to a lesser extent in Japan have sought to proactively increase their industrial partnering activities. This eagerness to partner has been driven, in part, by the realisation that collaborations with industry can be mutually beneficial, and in some cases by the decline in direct funding for research and teaching by governments. In the leading universities of the US, UK, and other industrialised countries, a decline in direct research funding during the 1990s has necessitated a search for new sources of funding and the adoption of new approaches to develop collaborative working relations with industry.

In the 1980s and 1990s, in relation to the US, Europe also experienced reduced investment in R&D and declining competitiveness of the pharmaceutical and other high technology industries, as evidenced by a lower expenditure on business R&D (as measured by the percentage of GDP allocated to these activities), a slower rate of increase in the number of new patents and lower university licensing revenues (http://www.oecd.org). Concerned with its declining competitiveness, the EU sought to create a "knowledge-based economy" through the Lisbon Agenda (http://www.ec.europa.eu/growthandjobs) by actively encouraging investment in R&D and partnering between universities, small businesses (such as biotech companies), and well-established R&D based companies.

An increase in such university collaborations began in the US with legislation to allow the commercial use of university research (Bayh Dole, 1980). A similar increase occurred in UK after 1986 when Government privatised agencies such as the National Research and Development Corporation (now BTG plc http://www.btgplc.com) and ownership of inventions arising from UK Universities could be commercialised by the inventing institution or in partnership with other organisations. This encouraged the creation of a large number of small companies in the BioPharma sector. By the end of 2003, there were around 1,830 companies in US and 1,484 companies in Europe which listed biotechnology as their primary activity (UKTI, 2005).

The UK Government has identified health sector as a key investment area and in 2003 commissioned a report on "Improving National Health, Increasing National Wealth" that mapped out sector investment priorities until 2015 with increased support for university knowledge-transfer groups (BIGT, 2003). Simultaneously in the UK, the Healthcare Industries Task Force was established to develop a closer working relationship between the government and the private sector with the aim of exploring issues of common interest and identifying opportunities for cooperation that would bring benefits for patients, health and social care services and industry (HITF, 2004). By 2005, UK was home to nearly half of Europe's publicly quoted biotechnology companies (UKTI, 2005). In spite of major government programmes to encourage university collaborations with these companies and substantial investment, very few studies explore the impact of these initiatives specifically analyse whether partnering has led to the achievement of the expected benefits or explore the nature and extent of these partnerships and the key issues faced by the partnering organisations.

In this paper we review the empirical research on R&D partnering in the BioPharma sector. Through primary research and using semi-structured interviews with key informants, we identify the nature of the partnerships formed and the key challenges faced by partnering institutions. We focus our study on partnering between universities and the pharmaceutical sector.

Innovation and Partnering in R&D

In addition to the "eureka" moments, innovation relies on the confluence of technology and knowledge. Schumpeter (1934) described innovation as "the carrying out of new combinations", arguing that breakthrough technologies occurred as a consequence of bringing together existing knowledge from different sources: a view shared by Dasgupta and Stiglitz (1980), who analysed the economics of industrial structures and the nature of innovative activity, and by Hargadon (2003), who argued that "breakthrough innovations come by recombining the people, ideas and objects of past technologies" and that "the future is already here — it is just unevenly distributed".

Partnering strategies to increase innovation in R&D

Technological information is a key output of R&D that may be used by firms to enhance productivity and market opportunity (Zeckhauser, 1996), and partnering enables access to this technological information.

Partnering strategies can be viewed from two perspectives. The first, a resource-based view of the firm, argues that its performance is a function of its ability to marshal internal resources that are difficult to imitate (Penrose, 1959; Wernerfelt, 1984; Teece, 1989). In the second, performance is viewed as a function of the competitive market and the firm's competitive environment in which it operates (Porter, M, 1980). A firm could enter into a partnering arrangement to enhance or complement its in-house capabilities or to improve its competitive environment.

Innovation requires knowledge, which may be acquired from R&D or market research, and the ability to implement and diffuse the arising ideas and inventions from this knowledge (Schumpeter, 1934; Dasgupta, and Stiglitz, 1980; Wernerfelt, 1984; Fiol, 1996; Kline, 2000; Hargadon, 2003). Partnering or outsourcing to access new technology allows the firm to gain internal leverage using external capabilities (Teece, 1986), and is seen by James (1994) as a key driver for structural change in an industry. Partnering can also help in other ways: by establishing social networks that facilitate collaborative learning (Burt, 1992; Cohen *et al.*, 2002); by providing access to emerging science and technology, as well as the necessary organisational capabilities (Powell, 1998); and by encouraging "open innovation" and "collaborating to compete". As Chesbrough (2003) argues, "the rise in excellence in university scientific research and the increasingly diffuse distribution of that research means that the knowledge monopolies built by the centralised R&D organisations of the twentieth century have ended".

The significance of the contribution to innovation by smaller companies was confirmed in 1999, when it was found that only 11.6% of US patents were awarded to the top 20 companies and almost 90% of innovation in R&D (as measured by patents) was in companies with small patent portfolios. Further, over 35% of all industrial R&D was performed by companies with less than 5,000 employees, as compared with 10% in 1981 (Chesbrough, 2003). In parallel, university-based R&D spending in the US doubled in real terms in the period 1970–1990 (Henderson *et al.*, 1994), and the number of patents awarded to universities increased from 250 in 1980 to over 1,500 in 2000 (Thursby and Kemp, 2002).

No coincidence therefore that in the 1980s, the traditional arm's length modes of interaction gave way to closer collaborations (Chiesa and Manzini, 1998) and between 1996 and 2000, globally, the number of pharma-biotech collaborations grew fourfold and by 2000 amounted to 160 alliances. By 2002, approximately 20% of pharmaceutical products were in-licensed from biotech companies (Richardson and Evangelista, 2002).

Partnerships have also helped to increase and improve the interaction of technical specialists from different disciplines, enable linkages of different groups with a common goal and transfer ideas from other industries (Teece, 1986; Burt, 1992; James, 1994; Cohen *et al*, 2002; Hargadon, 2003).

Universities that provide an accessible source of technical specialists across a broad range of disciplines are playing an increasing role in this respect (Thursby and Kemp, 2002; Chesbrough, 2003; Debackere and Veugelers, 2005). Internal partnering arrangements of different groups within a firm also enhance collaborative and cross-disciplinary working (Brown and Duguid, 2000; Reagens and Zuckerman, 2001).

Methods for decision-making

The literature shows that R&D investment decisions are increasingly shifting away from allocating resources to inputs, towards activities that optimise production of new knowledge (Ali *et al.*, 1993; Dushnitsky and Lenox, 2005). For successful R&D partnering effective allocation of resources requires careful selection of supplier, design of the product development process and management of the partnering project (Krishnan and Ulrich, 2001). Firms align their interests according to the individual product applications demanded by the market, the technologies available to them or according to their existing core competencies (Anderson and Nanus, 1991; Ali *et al.*, 1993; Brown and Eisenhardt, 1995; Granstrand *et al.*, 1997; Sharp, 1997). However, empirical evidence does not identify an obvious method for selecting suitable partners. Brown and Eisenhardt (1995) identify "trust, experience, appetite, power and influence to see the project through, access to relevant information and respect for you as a partner" as being important. Hargadon and Sutton (1997) highlight "critical mass, ability to enhance R&D capability and broaden product ranges, access to new technologies, potential for cost savings and focus on core competencies" as important factors taken into consideration when partnering.

Managing projects

We note that in partnerships, project management often focuses on assessment of financial performance, personal performance and development processes (Brown and Eisenhardt, 1995; Buckley and Chapman, 1998). Also, project success depends on the ability of the partnering organisations to assess the absorptive capacity of a firm; balance internal and external investment; make forward-looking decisions; communicate project goals to avoid inefficiencies and misunderstandings; overcome the "not invented here syndrome" (where partners are reluctant to support innovations from outside the firm); and rationalise management accounting systems to provide consistent data (Cohen and Levinthal, 1990; Damanpour, 1991; Brown, 1991; Ali *et al.*, 1993; Fiol, 1996; Kamien and Zang, 2000; Hargadon, 2003).

Organising for success

The experience of organisations acting as technology brokers suggests that partnering is facilitated by fluid organisational structures, flexible work practices, and communication of a shared sense of purpose and process (Hargadon, 2003).

Key organisational considerations for partnership success include creating the right environment for effective flow of "sticky" information between partners; establishing projects with sufficient technological overlap and acceptance of "innovation values" which allow a positive exchange between partners; overcoming the "not invented here syndrome" and the reluctance by partners to accept inputs or outputs of a third party; and selecting a project with sufficient strategic interest to ensure buy in at the highest level within the firm (Mowery, 1983; Van de Ven, 1993; Klein and Sorra, 1996; Zeckhauser, 1996; Mowery *et al.*, 1998).

In addition to the benefits intended directly from the partnership, a firm also gains unexpected benefits from spillovers: for example, transferring experience from one product development programme to another. However, a firm also experiences potential risks when sharing proprietary expertise as ideas and information may leak between partners (Richardson and Evangelista, 2002; Oxley and Sampson, 2004).

Unanswered questions relate to the optimal duration of the partnership and the proximity of partnering organisations in the value chain (Devlin and Bleackly, 1988;

Dasgupta and Stiglitz, 1980; Cantwell and Barrera, 1998; Cantwell and Iammarino, 2000; Oxley and Sampson, 2004).

Growing role of university partnerships

The increasing government spend on R&D in universities, improving record of successful intellectual property management, increasing management capability within universities to support industrial liaison and more flexible approaches to forming partnerships, have collectively made universities more attractive partners for industry (Jaffe, 1986; Jaffe, 1996; DTI, 2001, 2005; Lambert, 2003; Debackere and Veugelers, 2005). This has encouraged an increase in collaborative activities and for example, 77% of UK biotechnology companies now partner with one or more universities (Zeckhauser, 1996; Chesbrough, 2003; AUTM, 2005; UNICO, 2005; CBI, 2005).

A wide range of methods are used when partnering. These include defined contracts (activity-based), defined technologies (input-based), or defined strategies (output-based). Other than Debackere and Veugelers (2005) who have analysed how the role of technology transfer offices varies in Europe, to date, no studies have explored the nature of these partnerships in the context of R&D partnering between universities and industry. Hence, there is a gap in our knowledge of the nature of university–industry partnerships, what works and why, and the barriers and enablers of success, a finding which is surprising, given the substantial resources invested to encourage such partnerships which are mooted to be the engine of economic growth (DTI, 2004).

Methodology

Primary research for the study used qualitative method of inquiry and involved interviews with key informants using a topic guide which was piloted and iteratively refined before application (Mays and Pope, 1995). The interviews explored the nature of R&D collaborations and the extent of involvement in the partnering process for a diverse group of organisations.

We used theoretical (non-random) sampling over two stages (Strauss and Corbin, 1998). An initial set of key informants were "purposively" identified to capture a diverse group for the first stage of interviews. Additional key informants were further recruited by "snowballing" technique. Notes were recorded during the course of the interview and the research team reviewed findings in regular meetings to identify emerging themes, triangulate findings and identify saturation points when no new information was emerging. Data were grouped by emerging themes and iterative analyses allowed further categorisation of data by sub-themes derived from the main themes (Pope and Mays, 2000).

The 25 key informants included managers and scientists from large, medium sized and small pharmaceutical and biotechnology companies involved in collaborative research and development (GSK, Merck, Syngenta, J&J (USA), Abbott (USA), Tepnel Sciences and MicroTest Matrices); managers from technology transfer offices in major UK, European, and US universities (Imperial College London, University College London, Oxford, Dundee, MIT and Columbia); representatives from the venture capital and business angel financing communities; and Government officials from the UK Department of Trade and Industry (DTI). In the interviews we explored (1) strategies and structures adopted for partnering, (2) strategies for finding partners and choosing projects, and (3) factors which helped R&D partnerships work.

Data emerging from the interviews were augmented by further data collected through a questionnaire survey of university business development managers at 33 UK universities with technology transfer offices to explore their R&D partnering activities with industry. There were 20 respondents (a response rate of 65%). Data emerging from the survey was integrated with the interview findings for triangulation and thematic analysis.

Additional case material was collected from published sources to illustrate the partnership arrangements referred to by key informants.

Our study has certain limitations. We adopted a qualitative method and used theoretical rather than random sampling. To overcome these limitations we maintained a systematic approach to our research rigour at every stage of the study — in design, sampling, analysis and interpretation — with independent reflexive thematic analysis which allowed triangulation between team members (Mays and Pope, 1995). Our sample, though not statistically representative, was theoretically informed, relevant to the research questions and hence appropriate to our research.

Results

General partnering activities

Of the 20 universities interviewed or surveyed, 15 already had industry partners, with three stating that they were "nearly there" in terms of setting up new partnerships, and only two with no partnerships but "some leads". Amongst these, general levels of R&D partnering, as opposed to arm's length contracting, were increasing. However, only seven respondents felt their industry interactions were working well or very well, while nine respondents stated that they had mixed or little success to date.

Companies involved in R&D partnerships had a greater level of experience than their university partners, with some engaged in "about two dozen research collaboration agreements with academic institutions in the last five years". About half of the partnerships entered into by the companies involved in the study were local (UK), with the rest spread among many countries including US, Europe, and the Far East.

For one company, the total partnering budget in 2005 for preclinical collaboration projects amounted to £26.5 m. Another company had extensive partnering experience and the products from partnering underpinned revenues, with "38% of revenues arising from licensed-in products or technologies (particularly vaccines) and up to 50% of products dependent on licensed-in elements". In some cases, products had been developed through multiple partnerships. An example cited was the hepatitis vaccine developed by Merck & Co., which involved patent licenses from three universities and three companies covering elements such as constructs of viral protein, cell lines and adjuvants.

The academic Alternative Drug Discovery project at Imperial College (Imperial aADI) (Box 1) and the Kinase Consortium at Dundee University (Box 1) were specifically mentioned by a majority of those interviewed as being highly successful university–industry partnerships — the latter was considered by many of the key informants as the gold standard of pre-competitive research grouping.

Box 1. Examples of university industry R&D partnership structures.

Dundee Kinase Consortium

The University of Dundee's School of Life Sciences has been partnering with pharmaceutical companies since 1998 in a £20 million plus programme spanning 10 years, aimed at developing new drugs to fight serious illnesses such as diabetes, rheumatoid arthritis and cancer. The project was initiated to support Wellcome Trust-funded research and Scottish Enterprise-funded commercialisation activity in the laboratory of Professor Sir Philip Cohen, Director of the MRC protein phosphorylation unit. It has enabled Dundee to accumulate the largest collection in the world of drug targets, reagents and know-how relating to protein kinases and phosphatases (http://www.biodundee.co.uk press release of 31st March 2005).

GSK's Academic Alternative Discovery Initiative at Imperial

This collaborative research funding framework and alliance management agreement was initiated following introductory meetings between GSK and Imperial College London scientists in 2003. The aim is to increase innovation in GSK's R&D by offering a series of partnering opportunities along selected themes. The framework provides overarching agreement on IP terms, project costs and alliance management, together with terms of reference for the joint steering committee. Once GSK has allocated its annual budget for the programme, Imperial's university scientists are invited to meet with GSK's company scientists to identify potential areas of collaboration and present outline research proposals for screening by the Steering Group. Selected project proposals proceed through the GSK in-house planning process, facilitated by an alliance manager based at Imperial. As a result, GSK is able to tap into the multi-disciplinary science base at Imperial and Imperial receives additional funding and access to know-how for industrial drug discovery.

Pfizer Six Pack

Since the mid 1990s, Pfizer has enhanced its genomics drug discovery by collaborating with third party technology providers. By 2000, it had developed a "six pack" alliance hub with partners ArQule Inc. (ARQL, Medford, MA), Aurora Biosciences Corp. (ANSC, San Diego, CA), Celera Genomics Group (CRA, Rockville, MD), Evotec BioSystems AG (NMarkt:EVT, Hamburg, DE), Incyte Genomics Inc. (INCY, Palo Alto, CA) and Neurogen Corp. (NRGN, Branford, CT). Each partner brought expertise in early stage genetics and high throughput screening, such as ArQule's mapping array combinatorial chemistry libraries, to help Pfizer leverage its downstream drug development capability. The interactions also brought additional benefits such as opportunities for technology bundling and integration, training for staff and volume discounts on research reagents. This partnership strategy marked a significant shift for Pfizer in its approach to drug discovery, acknowledging the advantages of bringing ideas in from outside in terms of speed to market and increased innovation in its R&D (Zipkin, 2000).

Pipeline Deal Between Hoffman-La Roche and Antisoma

Hoffman-La Roche partnered with Antisoma Plc in 2003 at a cost of $43 million to gain access to its entire oncology product pipeline at all phases of development, along with all other Antisoma products moving into trials within 5 years. The agreement also includes options for Antisoma to buy back the rights to compounds with smaller market potential at various points during development (http://www.antisoma.co.uk).

Merck & Co.: Cancer Antibody Co-development Partnerships

Merck & Co., and Agensys recently announced they would collaborate on Pre-clinical and Phase I co-development and commercialisation of a novel therapeutic antibody for prostate cancer treatment. AGS-PSCA is an antibody that targets a prostate stem cell antigen and was discovered by UCLA scientists who later founded Agensys as they explored this target with the AGS-PSCA product. Merck & Co., also recently announced pre-clinical cancer collaborations with Vertex to develop and commercialise VX-680 and conduct joint research on Aurora Kinase inhibitors to identify drug candidates. These deals are worth around $200 and $350 million to Merck & Co., with initial upfront payments of $17.5 and $20 million respectively, reflecting the early stage of development of the technology (http://www.merck.com).

SNP Consortium

SNP consortium of pharmaceutical and bio-informatics companies, academic centres and The Wellcome Trust was launched in April 1999 to "develop and freely distribute a high density SNP map of the human genome" (Sykes, 2000, p. 74).

Varied partnerships

Overall, respondents reported that an increase in the number of BioPharma R&D partnerships has led to a wide range of variety of partnering arrangements. Many of these arrangements involve a reciprocal exchange of information and ideas, and extensive collaboration between partners. Many relationships are based on contractual relationships which use a framework approach definining inputs rather than outputs. Even material transfer or patent licensing contracts are rarely based on arm's length agreements. Instead, relationships tend to comprise a range of arrangements along a "partnership continuum" extending at one end from arm's length activities of transferring ready to use elements of a specific technology or piece of equipment (similar to a license or consultancy arrangement), to collaborative arrangements in which a partner undertakes a specified piece of work (depending on whether they have defined the outcome or the problem); to joint ventures designed to solve a problem using combined resources, including reciprocal "in-sourcing" arrangements (Fig. 2).

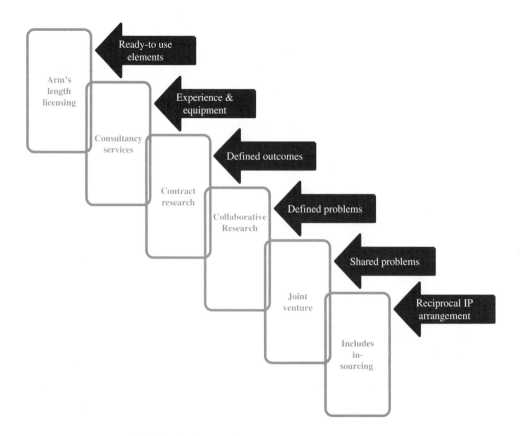

Fig. 2.   Continuum of BioPharma R&D partnerships.

Critical success factors for effective partnering

Detailed findings from the interviews and survey were grouped around five key emergent themes of (1) organisational structure; (2) operational management; (3) leadership; (4) developing organisational capabilities to improve partnering; and (5) creating an enabling environment for partnering.

Organisational structure

Respondents both from universities and industry stressed the importance of systematically and proactively searching for new R&D ideas to create partnering opportunities with external groups. Effective execution of this "search and select" function required appropriate organisational structures — such as specialist teams formed into dedicated business development units — to coordinate and support new R&D partnerships. In some cases these teams were sector-specific (such as those at Imperial and the Broad Institute which have dedicated teams for life sciences, physical sciences and so on): in other organisations team briefs were broader than one sector.

The majority of those involved in the study felt that universities were rapidly learning more corporate ways of organising their business development resources and were developing a critical mass of activity closely aligned with the areas defined in their research strategies. However, most of the informants noted an asymmetry between the supply and demand: the relatively early stage partnering opportunities available from universities outnumbered the later stage projects and programmes that partnering companies were more interested in.

Dedicated funding for establishing the commercial potential of early stage technologies (sometimes referred to as "proof of concept") featured strongly in our findings. UK universities reported "success" with their University Challenge seed funds. Companies were exploring how they could capitalise on this success and benefit from the new technologies emerging from universities by actively seeking opportunities to co-invest in technology development. Universities involved in the study had expanded their portfolio of investments by offering in-house proof-of-concept funds to finance development of technologies in other institutions.

An interesting finding was an arrangement where university research partners sub-contracted part of their research back to the industrial partner in an arm's length arrangement which could be considered as reverse-outsourcing — seen by some as "a sign of true partnership."

Theme-based networks or more formal structures, such as industry clubs and consortia, emerged as favoured modes of partnering for basic research. Although relatively few such clubs exist, the arrangement was popular amongst the universities and the companies involved in the study as it offered the opportunity of an "early view" of new technologies.

Operational management

All organisations involved in the study shared the opinion that bringing together groups from different disciplines helped to increase innovation in their R&D and enhance their ability to find innovative solutions to problems. But it was not possible to confirm this opinion with objective evidence.

Identifying new partners and new projects was described by university business development officers as a major activity. This activity involved networking (both internal and external), scouting for new projects (spotting opportunities), and sign-posting funding opportunities (finding funding). In addition, university business development officers were also involved in facilitating new partnering opportunities, closing deals and undertaking specialised tasks, such as managing IP, negotiating contracts, managing projects, corporate marketing, and training scientists in business matters.

Finding new partners and projects was considered by both university and industry informants as being particularly difficult. Various mechanisms were put in place by the organisations involved in the study to address this difficulty and to raise awareness of opportunities, including: making personal contacts in potential partnering organisations, setting up corporate web-pages inviting applications for technology development, involving external scientists as scientific advisors, publishing "hot-lists" of research needs, and undertaking systematic market intelligence based on publications and grant applications.

A number of company informants experienced difficulties in their partnering arrangements, especially the ability of universities to deliver on promises. In one case a university was described as "hard to do business with" because it took this institution nine months to prepare a term-sheet. In another, staff movements led to transfer of a project from one institution to another before the programme could be completed. A third experienced problems with the way projects were managed at the university, with excess bureaucracy and very limited resources to manage activities.

Many of the partnering difficulties cited by key informants typically arose from poor management of IP issues: either because partners were aware of their IP rights (but could not agree on how to share them); because they were uncertain of the IP that might emerge through the collaboration; or they did not know the best way to describe potential outputs of a project or apportion future IP streams emerging from the partnership.

In some cases, even when a partner was found and a suitable project identified, problems arose with resourcing the project, as the offer of partnership did not always result in an appropriate level of funding commensurate with resource needs. Both universities and companies found that they often needed to explore complimentary funding sources and assist each other with grant applications to secure additional finances.

There was uniform agreement of the key informants that the main tools for managing a partnership were legal contracts and progress reports. Contracts were seen as "a necessary evil to determine who owned what". Most preferred simple and straight-forward contract documents, The Astra-Merck model from 1982 was cited as a contracting option in which partnerships are treated as temporary arrangements organised around specific objectives. Another option identified was the more or less permanent framework of the Imperial-GSK aADI, which acts as an umbrella arrangement between these two organisations to encourage wide ranging interaction.

There was less agreement on how to measure success in a project or in a partnership arrangement. Some informants favoured outputs in a "milestone and deliverables" approach, while others preferred inputs, for example, in terms of the number of staff recruited and meetings attended. However, most agreed that a good approach was to "define the problem and then recognise when it is solved". An "open-book" approach, in which partners gained access to progress reports in order to satisfy themselves that the project was running to plan, was used to facilitate collaborative management of problems and the project. Others adopted a simpler measure of success, for example, recording whether their team would collaborate with a particular partner in the future.

In relation to success, an often cited difficulty was the difference in expectations from research, especially balancing "curiosity-driven" research in universities and more tightly planned basic developmental research in companies.

Other common partnering problems cited by informants related to difficulties in agreeing on a price for projects and in providing delivery incentives for the scientists.

Leadership

An important finding of the study, not identified in previous studies, was the importance placed on leaders within a partnership. Both companies and universities were keen to find project champions to support their initiatives and stressed the importance of supporting the right person with the ability to manage and complete projects. Generally, companies preferred to partner with people who demonstrated passion and commitment (not only competence and authority) and those with demonstrable communication skills.

It was felt that innovation in R&D could be enhanced by developing the leadership skills of key staff through training and by exposure to role models.

Strategically, it was considered important for partnership projects to be investigator-led — even when the decision to partner had been made at an executive level.

Developing organisational capabilities to improve partnering

Companies were keen to see a better standard of business development within universities so that they offered good value as collaborators. Specifically, companies were looking for scientific leaders (to do the research), experienced collaborators (to deal with contractual arrangements), and customer focussed individuals (to turn projects around quickly).

In terms of decision-making, company informants described a methodical approach to partnering which typically involved specialist input for the purpose of due diligence (consultants and literature reviews); an in-house project champion; and broader buy-in from other operational and executive functions. University informants on the other hand described a different approach to project development and partnering — one that began with a champion who first sought broader organisational buy-in, and then sought specialist advice for due diligence.

Company informants wanted universities to better understand the way industry operates, in order to enhance partnering opportunities and partnering success. Industrial fellowship schemes, which allow scientists to spend time in industry, were seen as a mechanism to increase this understanding, but in Europe such schemes are generally undersubscribed as there is less movement of scientists between universities and industry.

The companies interviewed believed that relationships with universities could be improved by increasing the speed of turnaround with contracts, citing that they were "not looking for a 'roll-over' but object to negotiators who are overly fussy". One informant cited that a university was "off the Christmas card list" because of unnecessary delays with contracting. But one university had improved relations with its partners by employing a more open approach to contracts and was enjoying more funding from the informant's company than any other UK university.

Several informants mentioned the benefits that might be obtained from an opportunity monitoring system which would offer access to ideas from a range of institutions (and preferably early insight into new opportunities) thus improving visibility of new projects and increasing the efficiency of partnering.

The concept of an internal technology scout or dedicated business development resource appeared frequently in interviews with both universities and companies, but company informants also identified a role for bigger groups with access to more funding and operational resources, such as web-based logs for project submissions and discretionary R&D funds.

Although many companies reported a large number of potential partners from which to pick and choose, they shared view that "good projects were hard to find".

Creating an enabling environment for partnering

Informants noted the growing government support for industrial R&D partnering activities both in the UK and other European countries, and cited a number of initiatives which illustrated the range of activities that supported partnering (Box 2).

However, the views of key informants on the adequacy of government support for partnering remained mixed. For example, one company informant observed that although he liked the recommendations of the Lambert Report, he felt the expectations were raised too high, commenting: "people don't seem to have read [the report] and some universities are aiming to raise too much money" from their licensing and partnering activities. Most agreed that it was still too early to see the full effect of these government interventions.

Box 2. Examples of State interventions to develop R&D partnerships.

NIH Protein Structure Initiative
In July 2005, the US National Institute of Health announced a $48.5 million award to Structural Genomix and the New York Structural Genomix Research Consortium to "produce proteins for structure determination for the collaboration" and provide access to crystallography facilities for its industrial and academic collaborators (http://www.scriptnews.com, 8 July 2005).

MédiTech Santé
July 2005 also brought news of the French Government's plan to create six world-class "poles of competitiveness" in a €1.5 billion knowledge transfer initiative, to include the MédiTech Santé health and biotech cluster in Paris and the Lyon-biopole vaccine and diagnostic cluster in the Rhone Valley. Both of these Bio-Pharma clusters are supported by companies such as Sanofi Aventis, Servier, GSK and Institut Pasteur (Paris) and BioMérieux, Sanofi-Pasteur, Merial and Du Puy/J&J (Lyon), together with a number of publicly funded research institutions. R&D partnerships are very much a part of these clusters, with the overall intent "to keep France in the forefront of pharmaceutical innovation and production" (http://www.scriptnews.com, 20 July 2005).

The London Biotechnology Network
The biotech community in London has seen the benefit of a series of networking meetings organised over the last three years in the form of the London Biotech-nology Network. These Wednesday evening meetings have been supported finan-cially by London's Development Agency and inward investment agency, London First, and have spawned an annual conference and exhibition held in December. The network provides firms with the opportunity to find out what is happening in the London area and meet potential partners in an informal environment free of charge for members (http://www.biolondon.org).

Overall, most respondents felt that UK and EU support for innovation in R&D was inadequate. Some UK initiatives were welcomed, and in particular DTI work-shops were identified as being "a good place to meet potential partners". The DTI micronano technology grants were also cited as having helped to attract investors for spin-out companies, because "having a feasibility study funded in-house gave a lot of confidence to potential investors". The venture capitalist interviewed shared the opinion that the [UK and European] government could do more, commenting: "It is really expensive doing phase two clinical trials for pharmaceutical products. Companies can't afford to run the trials from VC-funded equity investments [as there is not enough money in the system]". So how do companies fund more extensive trials? Some informants suggested that companies should partner with the NHS to develop cost-effective drugs or for universities to offer in-kind contributions in return for a future revenue share (although in practice such partnering may be very difficult to realise).

In particular, informants wanted the government to improve "the business climate for innovation, the fiscal regime for company investment in R&D, and planning permission for new premises". "By being prepared to support early stages of BioPharma research the government could support longer term innovation by providing a life-line to smaller companies and by strengthening the science base".

Companies viewed the R&D tax credits in the UK very favourably, as these "have provided a positive stimulation to the funding market", but would have preferred direct government grants to fund clinical trials. One informant suggested that it might "stifle innovation if governments cut back too far on their [health] spending — as they need to rebalance [drug] prices to protect the society".

Is R&D partnering working?

The final question on whether partnering has helped to increase innovation in R&D led to an overwhelmingly positive response from both companies and universities citing success. Overall, companies taking part in the study believed that partnering helped them to increase innovation in R&D, and led them to change their R&D structures to accommodate more open approaches to innovation to create better partnering opportunities with universities. However it was difficult to quantify this assertion, partly because there were few reliable methods for assessing successful outcomes other than launch of new products, an endeavour which typically can take up to 12 years due to the nature of R&D and innovation cycle in the BioPharma sector.

Should We Continue to Invest in this Area?

Although there is now more government funding for BioPharma R&D than previously — with the hope that this funding will stimulate partnering — asymmetry between business development capability in universities and companies has meant that concluding partnering deals has proved to be difficult. Much of the new business development resource in universities seems to be spent on networking (both internally and externally) in order to increase the number of partnering opportunities: an effort which often does not yield results. New tools and approaches are needed to assist in the identification of new partners and new projects.

The success in using relatively small amounts of "proof of concept funding" to stimulate innovative project proposals signals further potential to use this approach to stimulate new project proposals that could form the basis for future partnering programmes.

Conclusions

Competitiveness and technological leadership in the BioPharma sector is highly dependent on innovation which is expensive and high-risk. But in recent years, in spite of increased investment in research and development, the productivity of R&D in the BioPharma sector has declined. To counteract this decline in productivity, pharmaceutical companies have increased R&D partnering with a range of organisations — in particular with the university sector — to encourage innovation. Governments in the US and some European countries have encouraged this collaboration in research and knowledge transfer between universities and the pharmaceutical sector, as this sector is particular important to trade and the economy in knowledge-based economies.

Although there is a large body of literature on innovation in R&D and partnering, these studies have not explored partnering between universities and industry, an area that has attracted large amounts of state funding. There is a hence a big gap in our knowledge base. Our study which has explored partnering between BioPharma companies and universities aims to contribute to the knowledge base in this area.

Our findings show that universities are keen to undertake R&D partnerships to secure additional funding for R&D and inform their research. A range of partnership models have emerged in the UK that have actively supported future industry–university partnering. These partnership models are different to traditional arms-length approaches that involve one-off licencing or technology transfer but are rather long-term in nature, involving collaborative investment and development. There are early indications of success arising from collaborations encouraged by government sponsorship but there are no objective measures of this success or any attempts to date to measure this success in a systematic fashion.

Partnering with BioPharma companies for R&D has stimulated universities to augment their capabilities in a number of areas to better engage in these partnerships: for example establishing appropriate organisational structures to co-ordinate partnership approaches, strengthening operational management of R&D contracts, developing leadership, and developing more strategic approaches to managing R&D assets.

However, while partnering between universities and industry offers exciting opportunities, it also suffers from problems such as lack of adequate funding for the university teams; pressure on contract pricing from industry partners; asymmetry of knowledge and skills between the BioPharma organisations and universities that hamper partnering efforts; lack of administrative support from the university; problems with agreeing IP terms for technology transfer; and excessive university bureaucracy without adequate resources to address the bureaucratic barriers.

In spite of these problems industry–university partnerships are growing. The research identifies a number of critical success factors for these partnerships, which include:

Strong leadership. A leader, in the form of an internal project champion, is the most important success factor for the partnership. A leader is needed to communicate the aims and objectives of the R&D partnership to all the key stakeholders, to pick up an R&D project and make it happen, and to introduces new business practices to solve problems experienced by the partnership.

Developing two way interactions. In partnering projects there is evidence of emerging reciprocal relationships where groups provide specialist skills or resources needed for the project and two-way licencing of technologies to enhance research capability in both organisations involved in the partnership.

Improving organisational symmetry. Companies appear to be better prepared and resourced than universities to engage in partnerships. Often they have long experience of partnering and know-how in the execution of projects: skills that are lacking in many of the universities. Many companies, even if relatively new to R&D partnering, have well-established systems to support partnering and project management. Universities, on the other hand, are generally used to working with research councils and charities, hence their systems are not well organised to deal with commercial organisations. This misalignment leads to inefficiency in partnering and results in much frustration. This asymmetry in size and resources has been identified as an important barrier to partnering and novel structures may need to be considered (for example, multiple universities partnering in a consortium arrangement) to overcome this.

Partnership contracts and agreements. Difficulties are experienced in using traditional contracts to enforce R&D partnerships, especially where the inputs or the outputs may be uncertain. Better understanding of the potential pitfalls of traditional contract arrangements is critical to effective partnering and there is a need to develop partnering arrangements that are more conducive to the exchange of information and ideas (critically important in innovation) between the partners while ensuring intellectual property arising from these interactions are fairly shared. In particular it is important to develop partnership agreements that have transparent indicators of progress, in the form of deliverables and milestones, which are not used to hold hostage the partnering organisations but as an instrument to establish dialogue, collaboratively identify problems with progress and to jointly identify solutions to address these.

Developing metrics to measure success. We are unable to ascertain whether current partnering activities are making a difference. While the benefits of partnering are perceived, there is only a limited number of evaluations to demonstrate success of partnering. Given that the R&D lifecycle in the biotechnology and pharmaceutical industry often extends to 10–12 years before a product (the fruit of R&D) is launched, appropriate success measures along the innovation cycle need to be developed.

The study findings suggest an increase in industry–university partnering activities. The range and scope of these partnerships is evolving. Further operational research is needed to identify "what works and why" to inform future policies and better target scarce resources available for enhancing R&D.

References

Ali, A, AU Kalwani and D Kovenock (1993). Selecting product development projects: pioneering versus incremental innovation strategies. *Management Science*, 39(3), 255–274.

Anderson, JC and JA Nanus (1991). Partnering as a focused market strategy. *California Management Review*, 33(3), 95–114.

AUTM (2005). Annual survey of members. Available at URL: http://www.autm.org.

Bayh, Dole (1980) The Bayh-Dole Act: P.L. 96-517, Patent and Trademark Act Amendments, December 12, 1980. Available at URL: http://www.autm.net/aboutTT / aboutTT_bayhDoleAct.cfm.

BIGT (2003). *Bioscience 2015: Improving National Health, Increasing National Wealth.* Available at URL: DTI/Pub 6988/1k/11/03/NP. URN 03/1321 (available at http://www.bioindustry.org/bigtreport/).

Bottazzi, G, G Dosia, *et al.* (2001). Innovation and corporate growth in the evolution of the drug industry. *International Journal of Industrial Organization*, 19(7), 1161–1187.

Brown, JS (1991). Research that reinvents the corporation. *Best of Harvard Business Review.*

Brown, JS and P Duguid (2000). *The Social Life of Information.* Boston: Harvard Business School Press.

Brown, SL and KM Eisenhardt (1995). Product development: past research, present findings, and future directions. *Academy of Management Review* 20, 343–378.

Buckley, PJ and M Chapman (1998). The management of cooperative strategies in R&D and innovation programmes. *International Journal of the Economics of Business* 5(3), 369–381.

Burt, RS (1992). *Structural holes: The Social Structure of Competition*. Cambridge, MA: Harvard University Press.

Cantwell, J and P Barrera (1998). The localisation of corporate technological trajectories in the interwar cartels: cooperative learning versus an exchange of knowledge. *Economics of Innovation & New Technology*, 6(2/3), 257–291.

Cantwell, J and S Iammarino (2000). Multinational corporations and the location of technological innovation in the UK regions. *Regional Studies*, 34(4), 317–332.

CBI (2005). Industrial Trends Survey. Confederation of British Industry. Available at URL: http://www.cbi.or.uk.

Chesbrough, H (2003). *Open Innovation: The New Imperative for Creating and Profiting from Technology*. Boston: Harvard Business School Press.

Chiesa, V and R Manzini (1998). Organising for technological collaborations: a managerial perspective. In *R&D Management*. Oxford: Blackwell Publishing.

Child, J and D Faulkner (1998). *Strategies of Co-operation: Managing Alliances, Networks and Joint Ventures*. Oxford: Oxford University Press.

Cockburn, I and R Henderson (1996). Public–private interaction in pharmaceutical research. *Proceedings of the National Academy of Sciences of the United States of America*, 93 (23), 12725–12730.

Cohen, WM and DA Levinthal (1990). Absorptive capacity: a new perspective on learning and innovation. *Administrative Science Quarterly*, 35, 128–152.

Cohen, W, R Nelson and J Walsh (2002). Links and impacts: the influence of public research on industrial R&D. *Management Science*, 48(1), 1–23.

Damanpour, F (1991). Organizational innovation: a meta-analysis of effects of determinants and moderators. *Academy of Management Journal*, 34, 555–590.

Dasgupta, P and J Stiglitz (1980). Industrial structure and the nature of innovative activity. *The Economic Journal*, 90(358), 266–293.

Debackere, K and R Veugelers (2005). The role of academic technology transfer organizations in improving industry science links. *Research Policy*, 34(4), 321–342.

Devlin, G and M Bleackly (1988). Guidelines for success in strategic alliances. *International Journal of Strategic Management: Long Range Planning*, 21(5), 18–23.

DTI (2000). *Excellence and Opportunity — a Science and Innovation Policy for the 21st Century*. (CM4814). UK: Department for Trade and Industry. Available at URL: http://www.dti.gov.uk/ost.

DTI (2001). *Science and Innovation Strategy 2001*. UK: Department of Trade and Industry. Available at URL: http://www.dti.gov.uk/ost.

DTI (2003). Innovation report — competing in the global economy: the innovation challenge. URN 03/1607. Available at URL: http://www.dti.gov.uk/innovationreport/innovation-report-full.pdf.

DTI (2004). *BioScience Innovation and Growth*. UK: Department of Trade and Industry. Available at URL: http://www.dti.gov.uk/ost.

Dushnitsky, G and MJ Lenox (2005). When do firms undertake R&D by investing in new ventures? *Strategic Management Journal*, 26(10), 947–965.

FDA (2004). Innovation — innovation stagnation: challenge and opportunity on the critical path to new medical products. Available at URL: http://www.fda.gov/oc/ initiatives/criticalpath/whitepaper.pdf.

Fiol, CM (1996). Introduction to the special topic forum: squeezing harder doesn't always work: continuing the search for consistency in innovation research. *The Academy of Management Review*, 21(4), 1012–1021.

Gambardella, A, L Orsenigo and F Pammoli (2000). Global competitiveness in pharmaceuticals — a European perspective. Report prepared for the Enterprise Directorate-General of the European Commission.

Granstrand, O, P Patel and K Pavitt (1997). Multi-technology corporations: why they have "distributed" rather than "distinctive core" competencies. *California Management Review*, 39(4), 8–25.

Hargadon, A (2003). *How Breakthroughs Happen*. Boston: Harvard Business School Publishing Corporation.

Hargadon, A and R Sutton (1997). Technology brokering and innovation in a product development firm. *Administrative Science Quarterly*, 42(4), 716–749.

Henderson, R, A Jaffe and M Trajtenberg (1994). *Universities as a Source of Commercial Technology*: A Detailed Analysis of University patenting, 1965–1988. Cambridge MA: National Bureau of Economic Research (Working Paper No. 5068).

HITF (2004). Better healthcare through partnership: A programme for action. Report of the Health Industry Task Force co-chaired by Lord Warner and Sir Christopher O'Donnell. Available at URL: http://www.dti.go.uk.

Jaffe, AB (1986). Technological opportunity and spillovers of R&D: evidence from firms' patents, profits and market value. *American Economic Review*, 76, 984–1001.

Jaffe, AB (1996). Trends and patterns in research and development expenditures in the United States. *Proceedings of the National Academy of Sciences of the United States of America*, 93(23), 12658–12663.

James, BG (1994). The pharmaceutical industry in 2000: reinventing the pharmaceutical company. *The Economist Intelligence Unit*.

Kamien, MI and I Zang (2000). Meet me halfway: research joint ventures and absorptive capacity. *International Journal of Industrial Organization*, 18(7), 995–1012.

Kline, JJ (2000). Research joint ventures and the cost paradox. *International Journal of Industrial Organization*, 18(7), 1049–1065.

Krishnan, V and KT Ulrich (2001). Product development decisions: a review of the literature. *Management Science*, 47 (1), 1–21.

Lambert, R (2003). *Lambert Review of Business-University Collaboration*. London: HM Treasury. Available at URL: http://www.lambertreview.org.uk.

Lamoreaux, NR and KL Sokoloff (1996). Long-term change in the organization of inventive activity. *Proceedings of the National Academy of Sciences of the United States of America*, 93(23), 12686–12692.

Mays, N and C Pope (1995). Rigour and qualitative research. *British Medical Journal*, 311, 109–12.

Mowery, DC (1983). The relationship between intra-firm and contractual forms of industrial research in American manufacturing, 1900–1940. *Explorations in Economic History*, 20, 351–374.

Mowery, DC, JE Oxley and BS Silverman (1998). Technological overlap and interfirm cooperation: implications for the resource-based view of the firm. *Research Policy*, 27(5), 507–523.

Oxley, JE and RC Sampson (2004). The scope and governance of international R&D alliances. *Strategic Management Journal*, 25(8–9), 723–749.

Penrose, ET (1959). *The Theory of the Growth of the Firm*. New York: Wiley.

Piachaud, B and F Moustakis (2000). Is there a valid case for mergers within the defense and pharmaceutical industries? A qualitative analysis. *Journal of World Affairs and New Technology*, 3(4), 1–7.

Pope, C and N Mays (2000). Qualitative research in health care. Analysing qualitative data. *British Medial Journal*, 320, 114–116.

Porter, ME(1980). *Competitive Strategy*. New York: Free Press.

Powell, WW (1998). Learning from collaboration: knowledge and networks in the biotechnology and pharmaceutical industries. *California Management Review*, 40 (3), 228–240.

Reagans, R and EW Zuckerman (2001). Networks, diversity and productivity: the social capital of corporate R&D teams. *Organization Science*, 12, 502–517.

Schumpeter, J (1934). *The Theory of Economic Development*. Boston: Harvard University Press.

Sharp, M(1997). Outsourcing, organisational competitiveness and work. *Journal of Labour Research*, 18(4), 535–550.

Strauss, A and J Corbin (1998). *Basics of Qualitative Research Techniques and Procedures for Developing Grounded Theory*, 2nd Ed. London: Sage Publications.

Sykes, R (2000). *New Medicines, the Practice of Medicine, and Public Policy*. London: Nuffield Trust.

Taafe, P (1996). *Outsourcing in the Pharmaceutical Industry: The Growth of Contracted Services for Pharmaceutical Companies*. London: FT Healthcare.

Teece, DJ (1986). Profiting from technological innovation: implications for integration, collaboration, licensing and public policy. *Research Policy*, 15, 286–305.

Teece, DJ (1989). Technological change and the nature of the firm. In *Technical Change and Economic Theory*, G Dosi, Freeman C, Nelson R, *et al.* (eds.). London: Frances Pinter.

Thursby, J and S Kemp (2002). Growth and productive efficiency in university intellectual property licensing. *Research Policy*, 3(1), 109–124.

UKTI (2005). *Biotechnology Briefing Pack April 2005*. Presented to the DTI by Critical I Ltd in February 2005. Available at URL: http://www.uktradeinvest.gov/ukti/biotechnology.

UNICO (2005). *UK University Commercialisation Survey Financial Year 2004*. Available at URL: http://www.unico.org.uk.

Van de Ven, AH (1993). A community perspective on the emergence of innovations. *Journal of Engineering Technology and Management*, 10, 23–51.

Wernerfelt, B (1984). A resource-based view of the firm. *Strategic Management Journal* 5, 171–180.

Zeckhauser, R (1996). The challenge of contracting for technological information. *Proceedings of the National Academy of Sciences of the United States of America*, 93(23), 12,743–12,748.

Zipkin, I (2000). Industrializing expertise. Pfizer: Focussed Integration. BioCentury. July 24.

INDEX